Exploring Methodism

Methodist Theology

Thomas A. Langford

WIPF & STOCK · Eugene, Oregon

Wipf and Stock Publishers
199 W 8th Ave, Suite 3
Eugene, OR 97401

Methodist Theology
By Langford, Thomas A.
Copyright©1998 Methodist Publishing - Epworth Press
ISBN 13: 978-1-4982-0710-2
Publication date 1/15/2015
Previously published by Epworth Press, 1998

Methodist Theology

Contents

Preface to the Series

What is Methodism and how did it begin? What did John Wesley teach? We sing Charles Wesley's hymns but what can we discover about his life? What is the character and work of the Methodist Church today? What have Methodists had to say about social issues? What place have women had in Methodism? These are the kind of questions which *Exploring Methodism* is aiming to answer.

All of the contributors are experts in their field, and all write in an attractive way that will appeal to both church members and everyone interested in the life and history of the churches. The format of the books enables each writer to introduce extracts from the writings of the main characters and official church documents, and in this way to bring the reader close to what was actually said and written by the leaders of the church and church members. It is hoped that the books will be studied in house groups and other discussion groups as well as read by individuals, and questions for discussion, directly related to the present day, are included at the end of each chapter. Each volume contains an annotated list of books for further reading.

Barrie Tabraham opened the series with a general overview of Methodist history. He was followed by John Munsey Turner who traced the life and thinking of the Methodist Church from 1932 to the present day. For the present volume we welcome an American contributor, Thomas Langford, who explores the development of Methodist theology. Forthcoming volumes will cover the life and work of Charles Wesley, Methodist spirituality, music in Methodism, official statements by the Church on social and political issues, the activity of women in early Methodism, Methodist preachers and preaching, and other topics.

Foreword

Methodists are often thought to be the warm-hearted activists of ecumenism with not very much distinctive theology. While it cannot and should not be claimed that John Wesley was a Methodist equivalent of St Thomas Aquinas or John Calvin, nevertheless he was the great 'both . . . and' folk theologian who could combine 'protestant' biblicism with 'Catholic' sacramentalism without compromising either.

Thomas Langford interprets the ideology of the Methodists after Wesley from an American angle, introducing British readers to Nathan Bangs and Phoebe Palmer (who preached in England) and American readers (we hope) to William Arthur and William Burt Pope.

In our century American scholars have enriched our interpretation of the Wesleyan tradition. British scholars from the Methodist tradition have tended to be biblical scholars and rarely narrowly denominational. Langford astutely contrasts Rupert Davies seeking to reinterpret the creeds to contemporary people with Geoffrey Wainwright, seeking to introduce modern people to the richness of the creeds and the doctrine of the Trinity.

This book will be a boon to those doing courses on 'Methodism' in our colleges, though it is demanding at times. But I commend it wholeheartedly as an introduction to a rich cluster of traditions which are by no means dead.

John Munsey Turner

Introduction:

The British Methodist Tradition

Everyone is influenced by the inherited customs, beliefs and practices – in short, by the tradition – of the nation, community, church and family to which they belong. Awareness of this formative environment may be minimal, and perhaps the less it is recognized the more powerful its influence, but there can be no doubt that it nurtures, informs and sensitizes individuals, shaping their interests and values.

Tradition, however, is never simply accepted. It is constantly affirmed and criticized, extended and contracted, formed and re-formed. To live within the Methodist tradition, therefore, is both to inherit a way of thinking and acting and to share in an ongoing appraisal of its value and relevance. In the past, certainly, diverse views have been held together by common styles of worship, shared hymnody and corporate social and missionary activity, and thus family traits have persisted through times of apparently disruptive change.

To speak of the Methodist theological tradition is to refer to a process of learning and unlearning from predecessors, of retentions from the past and new developments. There is no over-riding and tight-fitting character and no unchanging essence. A better image is of a living body, held together by tendons of varying length and attachment, even as it bends, moves and grows.

Any attempt to describe a tradition imposes a form, in our case, a narrative form, on a selection of documents and persons. Thus, by making imaginative connections, a continuous account is created from discrete episodes. Inevitably, to choose materials for inclusion is also to exclude events and writings which others may regard as significant, and no interpretation can claim to be self-evidently correct in every respect. One hopes, however, that familiarity with the subject-matter will help a legitimate picture, making sense of the many books and ideas, to emerge. One hopes, too, that though this account is brief and impressionistic, it will evoke a sense of the character and quality of theology within the Methodist movement.

A tradition, then, is where we begin, and the nature of the tradition helps to determine where we will head. We tell our stories, in fact, to discover who we are and who we should be. Some traditions, moreover, direct towards openness, others towards closedness. Methodism has been an opening tradition, one which allows flexibility, exploration and new formulation. To be a Methodist, however, is also to have the resources of a special inheritance as we move into the future.

This theological genealogy, it should be explained, is traced not by an intimate member of the primary family but by a distant overseas cousin. I am an American United Methodist and look at British Methodism from that perspective. My survey reflects, therefore, both appreciation of and difference from the British tradition and lacks, inevitably, the thorough sensibility which comes only from being nurtured within the family. Nevertheless, it is presented with a sense of indebtedness and a desire to keep awareness of the tradition alive.

1

The Early Days

John Wesley

Fathoming John Wesley (1703–1791), the 'founder' of the Methodist movement, is as difficult as trying to capture water in the hand. He has been idolized and censured, appreciated and depreciated with equal vigour by historians, social critics, theologians and institutional leaders. This variety of view derives, in part, from the perspectives of those making the judgments. But Wesley's many-sidedness is also a source of difficulty. His interests and abilities were immense and his social impact, which has been evaluated in radically opposed ways, considerable. Moreover, his theological writings were occasional and unsystematic. In other words, he did not seek to achieve well-rounded, abstract, intrinsic completeness, but replied to pressing challenges, as they arose, in order to help those who had responded to his preaching.[1]

Theological style

Wesley's theological style was, in short, that of an active missioner. He worked out his theology in order to make his message, the message of one sent as an ambassador, as clear as possible. He can best be described, therefore, as a homiletical theologian, a service-oriented theologian, a practical theologian, and his ideas were framed as he stood in the presence of God and among the people of God.

Wesley's theological strength was drawn from his thorough grounding in scripture and tradition, espe-cially the tradition of the early (patristic) church; and he was spiritually formed by the lives of the saints and his own self-effacement and unswerving determination. It is hardly surprising, therefore, that he could reveal deep insights. But he could also be unexpectedly open to change and inconsistent under pressure! Wesley was neither easy to ignore nor easy to follow. He came upon his age like a juggernaut and moved across his century with a message [1] of shattering import.

---

1. If then sinful men find favour with God it is 'grace upon grace'. If God vouchsafe still to pour fresh blessings upon us, yea, the greatest of all blessings, salvation: what can we say to these things but, 'Thanks be to God for his unspeakable gift'! And thus it is. Herein 'God commendeth his love toward us in that, while we were yet sinners, Christ died' to save us. 'By grace,' then, 'are you saved through faith'. Grace is the source, faith the condition, of salvation.

Source: John Wesley, Sermon, 'Salvation by Faith'.

Practical divinity

Wesley's theology, then, is practical in nature and intention. It grew out of practice, was a reflection upon practice and aimed to enhance practice. It was for the shaping of life, and he rightly called it 'Practical Divinity'.[2]

The method of such theology is important. Wesley does not establish a theory, then apply it in practice. Rather, for him, interpretation arises from life situations and then rebounds to help shape new engagement with life. Knowing the truth comes by doing the truth; and knowing the truth reinforces doing the truth. In the theology of John Wesley, therefore, theology both derives from Christian experience and undergirds Christian experience. Practice and theory are held inseparably together. Each needs the other, and each enriches the other.

Moreover, practical theology, as Wesley understood it, is not identical with applicability, accommodation or sheer pragmatism. It has to do, rather, with theology belonging not to an élite but to the whole church and shaping life not according to dominant cultural patterns but in distinctively Christian ways. This original meaning should be borne in mind, in part as a corrective to later reinterpretations.

Theology and human need

Wesley's practical theology made him especially sensitive to human need in many contexts. Or, perhaps, his sensitivity to particular situations helped shape his practical theology. Either way, he was deeply convinced of Christian responsibility to serve the poor, to oppose slavery and smuggling, to establish educational institutions, to provide modestly-priced books to aid spiritual growth, to undertake mission activity and to identify with the needs of working people. Practical theology, for Wesley, was a means of being open to those in need and serving them in faithfulness to the gospel mandate.

Some interpreters, therefore, have argued that he was primarily concerned with the plight of the poor. The seriousness with which Wesley took the condition of poor people should certainly not be underestimated. It would be wrong, however, to give priority to any one of the social ills which he directly addressed. Nevertheless, precisely because Wesley's practical theology informed his preaching, his serving and his construction of theology, faith and works were, for him, inseparable in the Christian life. Practical

theology, in short, set a direction for the Methodist tradition.

A pre-Reformation legacy

Stephen Toulmin has argued that since the seventeenth century philosophy – and theology may be included – has been dominated by a 'theory centered' style, which poses problems, and frames solutions to them, in timeless and universal terms. In this way, Toulmin claims, half of the subject matter, belonging to the practical dimensions of life and thought, was left languishing and unaddressed. The spheres of the 'oral', the 'particular', the 'local', and the 'timely' were lost, and certainty rather than wisdom became the goal. This understanding of reason, Toulmin claims, must be challenged and practical philosophy must be rediscovered.[3] In the days when the search for 'wisdom' invigorated and guided philosophical interpretation, such practical concerns were certainly incorporated into much classical philosophy and theology. In a sense, therefore, Wesley was moving back to a pre-Reformation form of practical theology, and in this he brought new life to theological interpretation. Whether he deliberately chose this theological direction is not clear. But his awareness of the relation of Christian thought to Christian action is plain.

Theology and biography

Wesley's interest in the biographies of believers reveals another aspect of this practical theology. For him, life stories, simply and clearly presented, were the well-spring of both theological interpretation and guidance in Christian living. In the *Christian Library*, which he intended for the general education of Methodists, the majority of the fifty volumes are biographical accounts of saintly lives. In *The Arminian Magazine* [2] Wesley regularly included autobiographical statements from his preachers, subsequently collected in the *Lives of Early Methodist Preachers*. And this interest continued after Wesley in the *Methodist Magazine*, where approximately one-fifth of the material is biographical. Each year, moreover, the obituaries of ministers provided inspiration and uplift. This distinctive and creative use of biography reinforces the interplay of life as experienced and theological interpretation.

---

2. To the READER

1. A year ago I proposed 'To publish in what was entitled *The Arminian Magazine*, some of the most remarkable tracts on the Universal Love of GOD, and His willingness to save *all* men from *all* sin, which have been wrote in this and the last century, and to add some original pieces, wrote either directly on this subject, or on those which have a near relation to it.'

2. What I then promised, I have since performed in the best manner I was able. And I flatter myself that every sensible and impartial reader will allow, that the tracts already published are some of the best, if not the very best, that were wrote on the subject in the last century; at least, I shall be easily credited, when I affirm, that they are the best which ever came under my notice. And every one may see, that the writers were men of deep understanding, and perfect masters both of the arguments and of their own tempers.

3. I proposed to publish, in the second place, the lives of some persons, eminent for understanding and piety. I began with that of *Martin Luther*, wrote in *Latin*, and never published in *English* before. I went on with that of *Bernard Gilpin*, and then subjoined that of *Bishop Bedell*; three of the most eminent men whom God has raised up in *Europe* for several centuries.

4. To these I proposed to add a Collection of Letters, chiefly experimental. And as I had an immediate variety of these, perhaps greater than any person in *England* (not to say in *Europe*) I judged it most adviseable to select a few of them, such as I believed would be of most general use, and to place them in the order wherein they were written.

Source: John Wesley, *The Arminian Magazine*, January 1779, pp. iii, iv.

Preaching as theology

Gordon Rupp further illuminates the character of such practical theology when he points out that Wesley left a *kerygma* (sermons, preaching) rather than a creed. He did not attempt a systematic statement of Christian truth, but left sermons and *Notes on the New Testament* as guides to Christian understanding. Here, again, practice and theory, concrete engagement and intellectual reflection, are held tightly together. For practice needs to be guided by thought, and thought needs to be confirmed in practice if it is to continue to motivate.

Wesley and the Methodist ethos

John Wesley, as we have already noted, is an 'elusive' figure.[4] In discussing him, we have constantly to give and take back, state then qualify our statement, praise then modify our praise, criticize then rebalance our criticism. And all of this – which helps to explain the distinctive character of Methodism [3] – is as true of Wesley as a theologian as it is of Wesley as a church organizer, as a spiritual guide, as a writer of popular tracts or as a culturally important figure.

---

3. Here, then, are some of the reasons why the Methodists became distinct from the other evangelicals: the Arminianism of the Wesleys, their High Church, non-juring associations, their manysided spiritual inheritance, Protestant and Catholic, and the influence upon them of the Pietists and the Moravians. To these we must add the personal gifts and graces, the strength and weaknesses of the leaders of Methodism.

Source: E. Gordon Rupp in Rupert Davies and Gordon Rupp (eds), *A History of the Methodist Church in Great Britain*, Vol. I, Epworth Press 1965, p. xxxvi.

Salvation-centred theology

Nevertheless, there are basic things about Wesley's Christian thought which can be used as lode-stones to guide us in understanding him. In one sense, he was a true Anglican theologian: mediating, constantly counter-balancing extreme positions, seeking to find a middle way through challenging opposites. But, as with all mediating theologians, it is easy to charge him with lack of sharp definition and instability of position. There can be no doubt, however, about the persistent themes which run through his work.

From the beginning and throughout his development, Wesley's prime concern was with human salvation. From this centre he developed the most important emphases of his theology, like spokes extending from a hub. Salvation for Wesley was a comprehensive notion, including everything from the beginning of religious awareness to full Christian maturation and ultimate hope. Beginning with repentance, salvation was established by justification, affirmed by assurance, embodied in holiness and fulfilled in eternal life with God [4]. Through his life, from 1725 until his death in 1791, the stress laid on each of these themes varied from time to time, but taken together they represented the meaning of new life in God.

---

4. (A usual objection is)

That 'to preach salvation, or justification, by faith only is to preach against holiness and good works.' To which a short answer might be given: 'It would be so, if we spake, as some do, of a faith which was separate from these. But we speak of a faith which is not so, but productive of all good works, and all holiness.'

Source: John Wesley, Sermon, 'Salvation by Faith'.

Theological framework

Wesley, almost in passing, referred to scripture, tradition and reason, and later, experience, as the sources and framework of his theology. These sources have often been mentioned by interpreters, but Albert C. Outler drew them together explicitly and identified them as the Wesleyan 'quadrilateral'. Subsequently, they have become important points of reference in interpretations of Wesley.[5]

Scripture was undoubtedly the foundation upon which Wesley intended to build his interpretation of Christian faith. But scripture was always read through particular lenses: namely, tradition (of the Early Church, the Reformation and the Church of England), 'empirical' common sense (reason) and experience. For Wesley, however, there was no constant balance between them and, while scripture remained basic, the influence of these lenses on his exposition of specific doctrines varied over time.

There is the further complication that each lens is itself subject to re-interpretation. As 'reason', therefore, is given different meanings and 'experience' variously specified, the understanding of 'tradition' can change. This fluidity in the meaning of basic concepts has bequeathed problems as well as guidance to Wesley's followers. Nevertheless, John Wesley, who took many traditional doctrines for granted, resorted to scripture, to the tradition which had shaped him as an interpreter of scripture, to common sense informed by careful observation, and to (religious) experience, as he continually evaluated the ideas and actions of his followers and of those whose lives he revered.

Grace and free will

Theological discussion in the first years of the new movement concentrated on free grace and free will. The issue of free grace, which affected understanding of the availability of salvation for all people and of the moral character of God, was central. Wesley vigorously opposed interpretations of predestination, foreordination or election and, especially, reprobation or damnation, which depended upon God operating as omnipotence directed by omniscience. Both the mediatorial role of Jesus and the responsibility of human beings were, in his view, by-passed by such interpretations.

The character of God, Wesley passionately believed, was not that of a despot who arbitrarily chose some people for life and others for death. Rather, God's relation to human beings was expressed in Jesus Christ who called upon all people to repent and to respond in faith, for grace is free to all and free for all. 'Whosoever will may come' [5] was the repeated theme, and it was explored and expressed in extended discussions in *The Arminian Magazine*.

5.   Come, sinners, to the gospel feast,
       Let every soul be Jesus's guest;
            Ye need not one be left behind,
            For God has bidden all mankind.

       See him set forth before your eyes;
       Behold the bleeding sacrifice!
            His offered benefits embrace,
            And freely now be saved by grace.

Source: Charles Wesley in *Hymns and Psalms* (1983), no. 460, vv. 1 and 5.

6.

Kingswood, Oct. 30, 1748

Dear and Rev. Sir,
When I look back upon my past life, and see the directing and over-ruling hand of my gracious God, I am astonished, and cry out, Lord, what is man? and what am I? an ungrateful, rebellious worm, not worthy the ground I tread upon. Even in this last call of his Providence, how have I resisted, and mixed bitter draughts in my own cup, which the Lord never designed for me? But it was my perverseness and littleness of faith: I listened to the voice of the enemy, rather than the voice of God. I could not trust him, though he had been my refuge in every time of trouble. How did he gently strive to subdue my stubborn spirit, calming my fears, and shining in upon my soul with such clear, demonstrative light, that I could no longer withstand. I then rose up, and feebly followed the small still voice. I soon found obedience brings its own reward. My anxiety, my doubts and distrust all vanished, and a sweet calm succeeded, which has continued ever since. I know not what the Lord is about to do with me; but I am enabled to leave it all to him, O may I never again take the matter out of his great hand; but lay my body, soul, and spirit, all that I have and am, at his feet! O that he would make me a weaned child, simply looking up to him for all things.

Source: Mary Davey, *The Arminian Magazine*, January 1779, p. 41.

Throughout, the free grace of God was the primary and commanding emphasis, especially in its relationship to human freedom. The action of grace, counteracting the effects of original sin, made individuals both responsible for their personal sins – rejection of God and evil actions towards their neighbours – and free to respond to the love of God with gratitude and faith. The reality of the free grace of God was, by the early nineteenth century, so taken for granted that emphasis moved to the defence of human freedom; and this shift, as we will see later, had serious consequences for theological priorities.

Spiritual biographies

The Arminian Magazine, as we have noted, included spiritual biographies, increasingly contributed by ordinary people whose experience of life was closer to the readers than that of well-known Christians from previous times. They too [6] could bear testimony to the initiative of God's grace.

Main doctrines

On 17 June 1746 Wesley wrote to Thomas Church: 'Our main doctrines, which include all the rest, are three: that of repentance, of faith and of holiness. The first of these we account, as it were, the porch of religion; the next the door; the third, religion itself.' Wesley's controlling interests undoubtedly fell under these headings but their relationships proved difficult to define.

The chief tension was between faith and works. Faith, as expressed in repentance and justification, is a gift of grace; yet repentance is also a responsible human act and justification is made evident in good works. The interaction of the Divine and human, in other words, is always at the heart of the vital life of Christians. Moreover, like any personal relationship, the relation between God and human beings cannot be, for Wesley, either static or capable of mechanical explanation. Consequently, though the emphasis in his formulations may shift, sometimes on God's initiative, sometimes on man's response, grace is always [7] the dynamic, underlying reality.

7. 'What then is the mark? Who is a Methodist, according to your own account?' I answer: A Methodist is one who has 'the love of God shed abroad in his heart by the Holy Ghost given unto him', one who 'loves the Lord his God with all his heart, and with all his soul, and with all his mind, and with all his strength'. God is the joy of his heart, and the desire of his soul; which is constantly crying out, 'Whom have I in heaven but thee? and there is none upon earth that I desire beside thee! My God and my all! Thou art the strength of my heart, and my portion for ever!'

Source: John Wesley, *The Character of a Methodist*, 1739.

John Fletcher: A Theological Colleague

In spite of his strengths and seeming self-sufficiency, John Wesley was helped by the contributions of colleagues and, in theology, he was especially indebted to John Fletcher (Jean Guillaume de la Flechere, 1729–1785). For example, Wesley struggled repeatedly, as we have seen, with the tension between graciously evoked faith and human responsibility. But he never achieved the statement of a position which satisfied either those who argued for 'grace alone' or those who believed that 'good works' are a necessary component of Christian salvation.

In the Methodist Conference of 1770 Wesley made another attempt. In retrospect, it was judged to be too hasty and too carelessly formulated. Nevertheless, the statement was made, and was immediately challenged.[6]

Checks to Antinomianism

John Fletcher came to Wesley's defence [8], and in the next eight years wrote a thorough and carefully constructed theological exposition. He entitled his work, *Checks to Antinomianism*. The title is important, since Fletcher's defence was addressed, in part, to those who believed that, if people are saved by grace alone, they have every excuse to do whatever they wish and still expect to receive God's salvation. The

work is also directed at those Calvinists who, Fletcher believed, did not provide an adequate place for good works in their interpretation of salvation.

8. Thinking it therefore safest not to 'put asunder' the truths which 'God has joined together', he [John Wesley] makes all extremes meet in one blessed Scriptural medium. With all Antinomians he preaches, 'God worketh in you both to will and to do of his good pleasure'; and with the Legalist he cries, 'Work out, therefore, your own salvation with fear and trembling', and thus he has all St Paul's doctrine. With the Ranter he says, 'God has chosen you, you are elect'; but, as it is 'through sanctification of the Spirit and belief of the truth', with the disciples of Moses he infers, 'make your calling and election sure, for if ye do these things ye shall never fall'. Thus he presents his hearers with all St Peter's system of truth, which the others had rent to pieces.

Source: John Fletcher, 'The First Check of Antinomianism', *The Works of the Reverend John Fletcher*, I, p. 37.

Fletcher's qualifications

John Fletcher was a good man to come to Wesley's aid. He was saintly, perhaps the most revered man within the larger Methodist movement, and well trained to carry the theological torch. As a result, he could enter even a tense debate with good will and the desire and ability to state the issues clearly and discuss them fairly.

Fletcher had come to England from his native Switzerland. He had already received theological training but did not enter the ordained ministry in his homeland. After moving to England, he was deeply affected by the Methodist movement and, with the prompting of John Wesley, became an ordained priest in the Church of England. He served the parish in Madeley, Shropshire, and in the last years of his life was married to Mary Bosanquet, who was also extolled as a remarkable example of holiness.

Convinced that Wesley would be misunderstood if the 1770 minutes were taken as his definitive statement, Fletcher attempted to set the discussion of grace and works in a larger context. In doing so he not only spelled out Wesley's thought more adequately but also added his own perspective which, while in harmony with Wesley's, yielded fresh insights.

Fletcher's approach

Having stated his basic perspective tersely [9], Fletcher spelled out its implications. He began by

---

9. The error of rigid Calvinists centres in the denial of that evangelical liberty, whereby all men, under various dispensations of grace, may without necessity choose life. And the error of rigid Arminians consists in not paying a cheerful homage to redeeming grace, for all the liberty and power which we have to choose life, and to work righteousness since the fall.

To avoid equally these two extremes, we need only follow the Scripture-doctrine of free-will restored and assisted by free-grace.

Source: John Fletcher, 'On Reconciliation', *Checks to Antinomianism*, New York: J. Collard, 1837, Vol. 2, pp. 333–34.

---

stressing God's action in history and the particular ways God actually relates to human beings. He refused to speak abstractly about God's sovereignty or will, focussing rather on the age of Jesus Christ, when God was historically present in person, and on the age of the Holy Spirit, in which God has acted in special ways since Pentecost. Fletcher's theology is thus relational and abandons any attempt to discuss God apart from the modes of God's historical presence. In this interpretation he clearly helped John Wesley to say what he had been striving to say [10]; and, from this time, Wesley utilizes Fletcher's formulations.

Fletcher holds together God's initiating and supporting grace, on the one hand, and human ability to respond and participate in God's gracious self-offering, on the other. God's grace is primary, originative, supporting and fulfilling. And God, as grace, has final purposes for history and the total human enterprise.

---

10. Thus he [John Wesley] advances God's glory every way entirely ascribing to his mercy and grace all the salvation of the elect; and completely freeing him from the blame of directly or indirectly hanging the millstone of damnation about the neck of the reprobate. And this he effectually does, by showing that the former owe all they are, and all they have, to creating, preserving, and redeeming love, whose innumerable bounties they freely and continually receive; and that their rejection of the latter has absolutely no cause but their obstinate rejecting of that astonishing mercy which wept over Jerusalem, and prayed, and bled even for those that shed the atoning blood – the blood that expiated all sin but that of final unbelief.

Source: John Fletcher, 'The First Check to Antinomianism', *The Works of The Reverend John Fletcher*, I, p.38.

Nonetheless, grace gives and nurtures human freedom, and undergirds human responsibility to respond to God and to express holiness in life. God has expressed sovereignty through self-limitation by creating and endorsing human freedom, freedom which is truly exercised in response to God. Consequently, for Fletcher, as for Wesley, all is of grace and grace, being grace, respects human integrity as it meets human life.

The historical meeting of God and human beings is the base for Fletcher's affirmation of the 'moral' character of God. God could not manipulate human beings, disregarding human worth; he could only treat them as persons to be addressed, won, and made responsible. This view was in contrast to what was often taken to be the 'immoral' character of Calvin's God, that is, a God who acts in a despotic, independent, or deterministic manner [11]. In agreement with Wesley, Fletcher presents God in terms of a dynamic love which evokes love both to God and neighbour.

David C. Shipley has drawn Fletcher's themes together:[7]

1. Man is utterly dependent upon God's free gift of salvation, which cannot be earned but only received; and

2. The Christian religion is of a personal and moral

11. On Reading the CHECKS and other Polemical Works of Mr. FLETCHER

When zeal impetuous urg'd her vot'ries on
To force submission to great *Calvin's* throne,
With fire unhallow'd glowing in her breast,
She cries aloud, '*Protest*, my friends, Protest!'.
Wisdom in guise of peaceful *Fletcher* came,
And check'd her rage, and stopped the spreading flame;
His pencil gives fair Truth her robes of light,
While vanquish'd Error flies to shades of night.

Source: unsigned poem in *The Arminian Magazine*, January 1779, p. 47.

character involving ethical demands on man and implying both human ability and human responsibility.

A key issue

The most vexing issue and one which required the most careful handling was: in what ways do ethical demands imply human ability? By contrast with the Enlightenment, Fletcher always insisted that moral activity does not express a native capacity but reflects a graciously given endowment, an endowment that, though blighted by sin, has been graciously restored by God's continuing ministration through the Holy Spirit. Both original sin and justification by grace are affirmed, but sinful human beings are not left deprived of God's grace. Consequently, in the event of human salvation, grace meets grace as it is refracted through human response and responsibility.

Centrality of holiness

Fletcher, also with Wesley, made holiness the true end of Christian life. For him, the immediate presence of the Holy Spirit, when fully accepted, meant the closest loving interaction between God and persons, and he refers to this as the baptism of the Holy Spirit. His primary concern is thus to make clear the immediate, loving relationship of God with human beings. There

is no formula or exact mould into which this relationship must fit. But God never infringes human integrity, and his grace and the wills of individuals interact to produce responses appropriate to specific times, needs and possibilities. And the goal is always the realization of perfect love in the believer.

The gracious Trinity

For Wesley, grace was the expression of God's primal character, defined in Jesus Christ and conveyed by the Holy Spirit, and this link with the Holy Trinity is affirmed by Methodist contemporaries like Charles Perronet [12]. In recent decades, the importance of grace as the fundamental Wesley motif has been underlined,[8] and Albert C. Outler has lately described this theme with his typical conciseness and energetic style:

At the heart of our Wesleyan legacy is an ample spirit of grace – the grace of our Lord Jesus Christ which is the love of God manifest in the koinonia of the Holy Spirit – and this has given us the core of whatever consensus we have ever had or can hope for in the times ahead. Any such consensus must allow for variety in formulation; it must require an unfeigned acknowledgment of its imperatives to holiness – the love of God and neighbour. The need for grace is radical, the offer of grace is real, the gift of grace is consummate in Jesus Christ, the giver of grace is the Holy Spirit (Lord and Life-Giver!). The community of grace is our shared koinonia in the Body of Christ joined to the Head and to itself through its 'members'. The reception of free grace is by true repentance and faith, the rule of grace is the Rule of God, the sign of grace is grateful self-giving love, the tasks of grace are defined by human wretchedness and need, the confidence of grace is that nothing in all creation can separate us from the love of God in Christ Jesus, our Lord.[9]

There are several emphases which need to be spelled out. First, and most important, is God's presentation of the divine character in Jesus Christ. For Wesley,

12. Each *Divine Person* vouchsafes to bear a peculiar relation to us, affirms a peculiar character, and acts a different part in our redemption. God is undivided in his Essence, but distinct in Personality; and what in one part of Scripture is ascribed to the undivided God-head, is in other parts ascribed separately to each person. The Son sends forth *Grace*; which implies the whole of our Redemption, Pardon, and Holiness; all *purchased forever*. The Father sheds abroad his Love, opposite to the wrath which is due to disobedience. The Spirit vouchsafes *Communion*, which through his agency we receive with the Father and the Son. And this Communion is opposed to *Separation* from God.

Source: Charles Perronet, *The Arminian Magazine*, April 1779, p. 200.

grace is a person – Jesus Christ – and is always personal in its expression. What is true of the Godhead is expressed in continuing creation, is exhibited in the person of Jesus and is enlivened by the Holy Spirit. This is a distinctive Wesleyan emphasis: God is alive and vital as grace.

Second, grace has its mode of being in 'prevenience'. In other words, God, who has taken the initiative in the past, continues to move prior to human awareness, always going before and preparing the way for human action. This is the nature of the Trinity and is expressed in creation, initial salvation, and maturation.

In recent interpretations of Wesley, the primacy of the Trinity is maintained, but there are different weightings of emphasis. Geoffrey Wainwright tends to stress the entire Trinity, while Thomas Langford has emphasized the centrality of christology and Albert Outler has underlined the role of the Holy Spirit in a 'trinitarian pneumatology'.[10] In short, even as Wesley's trinitarian base is recognized and affirmed, his precise position is variously understood.

Third, grace enjoins mission: for grace evokes gratitude and benevolence, exhibited in the gracious sharing of grace. To participate in the 'mind of Christ', to be a part of 'the body of Christ', is to share grace even as 'Christ for our sakes' was grace.

In this movement, in these extensions from the centre, are located the grasp of grace and the reach of grace. But a word of caution and clarification needs to be spoken. In contemporary sensibility, grace carries overtones of softness, of passiveness, of easy forgiveness or quiet overlooking, of being sentimental, nonjudgmental, sweet and amenable. But for Wesley grace was exhibited on a cross and carried the character of judgment, opposition, and rehabilitative hope as well as justification, forgiveness and the formation of new life.

John Wesley and the Enlightenment

It is fundamental and generally agreed that John Wesley's primary theological indebtedness was to scripture, to his own Anglican tradition and to the early church. His particular cultural and intellectual setting, however, was also significant. Consequently, in appreciating the theology of John Wesley it is important to note that the eighteenth-century revivals were the first major religious movements in Europe after the Enlightenment.

Characteristics of the Enlightenment

The Enlightenment was a generalized intellectual movement in Europe, particularly represented in Great Britain by Isaac Newton, but extending through British intellectual developments from Bacon to Locke, to Hume and to Toland. In France it found clear expression in, for instance, the work of Voltaire and Rousseau; and in Germany there was special culmination in the philosophy of Immanuel Kant. With all of these thinkers, achievements in the physical sciencies were applied to the realm of human intelligence and action. Enlightenment sensibilities provided a general cultural ethos or intellectual awareness for Wesley and constituted an ambience for the development of some of his themes. Several aspects of this situation are significant.

Reformation and Enlightenment

As background, we need to recognize that the Enlightenment sharply separated the eighteenth-century British intellectual context from that of the sixteenth-century European Protestant Reformation. The Reformation was a struggle among Christians who shared many common assumptions inherited from classical Christianity: for example, belief in God, in the value of scripture, in the deity of Jesus Christ, in Christian morality, etc. The Reformation was an internecine battle; it was waged among Christians who sought the most authentic ways of expressing their faith. The Enlightenment, in contrast, questioned every received authority, including the active sovereignty of God. Autonomous, rational human beings were enthroned as the valuers of reality. Consequently, Wesley faced a world increasingly infected by denial of Christian values and by active opposition to received theological convictions. There was a new opponent, indeed enemy, in the post-Enlightenment era.

Wesley's response

Wesley responded both in opposition to and in agreement with the Enlightenment. In opposition to the Enlightenment's conviction that human nature is good and that a natural religious awareness is native to all people, Wesley forthrightly emphasized original sin and the destitute character of human life. His sharp concern about sin, and therefore his battle with an Enlightenment presupposition, helped to differentiate his emphasis on salvation from the looser concerns of the Anglican church of his day.

Similarly, Wesley's emphasis on Christian perfection, derived from ancient Christian understanding and Roman Catholic piety, was also a corrective of Enlightenment belief – in this case, in human perfectability. Wesley stressed that, though both sides aspired to complete fulfilment, the Christian hope for full salvation, unlike that of the Enlightenment, sprang from confidence in God rather than self-confidence.

At the same time, Wesley's recognition of the necessity of human response in the Divine-human relationship must be set within the Enlightenment ethos. Human freedom and therefore the natural possibility of human response to God could not simply be set aside, as Luther and Calvin had tended to do. There was an issue which needed to be faced, and Wesley tried to face it. As we have seen, the character and basis of human 'response-ability' was a permeative problem throughout his theological reflections. It was his opposition to the Enlightenment, especially to Newton and Hartley, that guided his opposition to predestination. In his denial of mechanistic interpretations of action, as found in *Thoughts upon Necessity*, 1774, he sought to find a way to deal with the distinctiveness of human thought and action. It was precisely at this point that John Fletcher came to his assistance.

Finally, Wesley's ecumenical attitudes may be seen, in part, as a response to the Enlightenment. The need to respond to an outside threat prompted Christian groups to abandon intra-ecclesiastical debate and to stand with fellow believers, despite theological differences, in order to witness to Christian faith.

Again, in stressing the Enlightenment cultural ambience in which Wesley lived, we should make clear that we are speaking about ideas and assumptions which were in the air rather than about a dogmatic system. Such notions, however, affected British and European culture and, as such, constituted an atmosphere which Wesley breathed and by which his own sensibilities were formed.

John Wesley on church and sacraments

Martin Schmidt has asserted that for John Wesley the notion of church equals mission. And this, he claims, is distinctive in Christian history.[11] At one level, Wesley never questioned the legitimacy of the Church of England, and he accepted its ministerial orders as a representation of a valid church order. Yet he also went beyond the *status quo* by never claiming that it was the only valid order or that its way of working could not be challenged. In a basic sense, Wesley was not deeply interested in changing the organization of the church. He was interested in extending its life through unrestricted preaching beyond the church buildings and small group fellowship within its life. In many things, Wesley was conservative and willing to live within the inherited order. At the same time, he was pushing the boundaries of that order to enlarge Christian witness and to promote Christian nurture. It is unclear whether Wesley failed to realize the implications of what he did, or acted accepting them, or simply did not look, being indifferent to the issues, beyond his immediate convictions about what needed to be done. In any case, Wesley pursued his sense of mission to preach salvation and holiness. This was, he believed, the fundamental task of the church, and the church was authentic as it pursued it.

Wesley fully participated in the sacramental life of the Anglican church, and he stressed the importance of sacraments as means of grace [13]. But Wesley should not be interpreted primarily in terms of his faithful observance of the rituals of the church. He was, in this as in all other things, exceedingly practical and specific. For him, Christian commitment found expression in the habits and structures of daily living. Hence, participation in worship was a duty owed to God, and it shaped communion with God. The

sacraments were the historical embodiment of Divine-human relationship, and the use of other means, such as prayer, scripture study, fasting, and meeting in Christian community, was also important in the daily renewal of the life of faith.

Wesley never spoke of the church in abstract terms. Participation in worship, the life of fellowship and diligent use of the means of grace were always related to the actual moulding of Christian character. Wesley's pietism was not primarily self-attention or simply a means of self-improvement but a thankful response to God's gracious action. Wesley deeply believed that living according to the two great commandments results in profound happiness. For to be religious is to practise those disciplines and to enjoy those interactions which express and enhance a person's relationship with God. And from daily communion with God comes joy.

Wesley's understanding of the church came from participation in the life of the church, and his understanding of the means of grace derived from sharing in them. For him practice and theory were deeply interrelated, each needing and supporting the other. Theology was practical; Christian thought was partner with Christian living.

The openness and practicality of Wesley's understanding of the church were illustrated by his continuing refusal to leave the Church of England and by his establishment of a new church in North America. In England, the Anglican church was the accepted context of religious life and, even though after Wesley's death Methodism emerged as a separate body, he did not himself accept the necessity of an independent ecclesiastical institution. He seemed convinced, on the other hand, that in North America an independent church would be valuable and sanctioned its establishment.

Assessment of Wesley as a theologian

Assessment of Wesley as a theologian is difficult, and perhaps unnecessary. There are at least two problems: 'theology' is a difficult term to define and Wesley's precise contribution to it is hard to identify.

13.　O the depth of love divine,
　　Th' unfathomable grace!
　　Who shall say how bread and wine
　　God into man conveys.
　　How the bread his flesh imparts,
　　How the wine transmits his blood,
　　Fills his faithful people's hearts,
　　With all the life of God?

　　Sure and real is the grace,
　　The manner be unknown;
　　Only meet us in thy ways
　　And perfect us in one.
　　Let us taste the heavenly powers:
　　Lord, we ask for nothing more.
　　Thine to bless, 'tis only ours
　　To wonder and adore.

Source: Taken from Charles and John Wesley, *Hymns on the Lord's Supper*, 1745.

It is clear, however, that Wesley was not a theologian of the classical Protestant or Scholastic type. Equally, he was not, and did not want to be, a thinker who steps back from the world in order to reinterpret it. Rather, he functioned through his Christian engagement with life, and held theory and practice tightly together. Simply because this approach was very different from Roman Catholic and Protestant confessionalism, both of which stressed creeds and dogmatic definitions, he had difficulty in being consistently clear about what he was doing and articulating it. For him, theology grew out of and informed Christian life.

Charles Wesley: theology-as-hymn

This account of Methodist theology has made John Wesley the chief fountainhead of the movement and its theology. That John Wesley was the major initiator and shaper of the Methodist revival movement is not in doubt; he assumed and asserted leadership. But is it equally clear that he was the sole or even the most important source of theology within this tradition? Some important commentators have been doubtful and have wanted to affirm the role of Charles Wesley (1707–1788), the brother of John, as the major figure in shaping Methodist theology. For example, E. H. Sugden has claimed that, 'the real embodiment of Methodist theology is the Methodist hymnbook and especially Charles Wesley's hymns'.[12] J. E. Rattenbury has stated forthrightly, 'It is certainly true that his, Charles' and not John's, was the most effective and comprehensive statement of Methodist doctrine.'[13] Franz Hildebrandt, who was convinced of Charles' primacy, claims that the hymnbook is 'Wesley's doctrine', and that the hymns provide 'a basis for the summa of Charles Wesley's theology'.[14]

These claims must be taken seriously because of the stature of the commentators, and it is certainly the case that the hymns provided a remarkable and inclusive statement of Methodist beliefs. Hymn singing, moreover, was distinctive of the revival movements of the eighteenth century. As the opening sentence of the preface to the 1933 British Methodist hymnbook says, 'Methodism was born in song' – and Charles Wesley's hymns made Methodist theology memorable.

In such hymns [14], theology is not and does not appear as an intellectual discipline but finds expression in acts of worship, praise and commitment. Methodists, in short, were expected to sing what they believed and believe what they sang. Here, indeed, was practical divinity, and here John and Charles are at one.

---

14.   Thy sanctifying Spirit pour
              To quench my thirst and wash me clean:
        Now, Father, let the gracious shower
              Descend and make me pure from sin.

        Give me a new, a perfect heart,
              From doubt, and fear, and sorrow free:
        The mind which was in Christ impart,
              And let my spirit cleave to thee.

Source: Charles Wesley, in *Hymns and Psalms*, Methodist Publishing House 1983, no. 726, vv. 3 and 4.

Content of hymns?

For our purposes we need also to ask, what was the content of Charles Wesley's hymns? The emphases were the same as John's, and herein lies a problem. For the hymns of Charles were edited by John, and it is difficult, if not impossible, precisely to separate their several contributions. Plainly, however, Charles' hymns made human salvation central: he spoke clearly of human sin and justifying and sanctifying grace. It is no accident, therefore, that 'Love Divine, all loves excelling', has probably remained his favourite hymn among Methodists. But there is another problem. The total collection of hymns is arranged as a spiritual biography of a 'true Christian', according to the Wesleys' understanding. Consequently, it touches upon the entire range of Christian experience, and the precise emphases of Charles' hymns may be obscured by John's arrangement. It is John's prose that orders Charles' poetry. But at every point the theology is experience-based.

Though there may be, from time to time, differences of emphasis – in his later hymns, for example, Charles tended to stress the process of growth towards perfect love rather than its instantaneous gift – fundamentally there is no conflict in substance between the theology of the two brothers [15]. For both, religion is

---

15.   Thy sovereign grace to all extends
            Immense and unconfined;
        From age to age it never ends;
            It reaches all mankind.

        Throughout the world its breadth is known,
            Wide as Infinity!
        So wide, it never passed by one,
            Or had it passed by me.

Source: Charles Wesley, in *Hymns and Psalms*, Methodist Publishing House 1983, no. 46, vv. 2 and 3.

---

experiential, scriptural and personal, and, for both, these qualities underlie their theological statements. It might seem unfair, and perhaps disingenuous, therefore, to credit either one with the chief role in shaping theology in the Methodist tradition. But because of John's presumptive role as leader, because of his capacity to order emphases and because of his quick willingness to edit Charles' work, we have ascribed to him the primary place. More important, perhaps, is the recognition of the joint influence and the common contribution which these two brothers made to the formation of Methodist theology.[15]

The Wesleys gave both impetus and structure to the

Methodist movement. The dynamic of their concern for preaching and nurture, for practice and thought, for mission and personal benevolence was rooted in the triune God of grace and in responsive, grace-filled living. The theology of the movement was a part of the movement: the movement gave rise to theology and theology undergirded the worship, the singing, the preaching and the mission of the movement. Neither the movement nor its theology could be understood separated from one another. Thought and life were intrinsically bound to one another. Yet, as we shall see, these characteristics were so distinctive as to be difficult to convey or maintain.

For discussion

1. What do you think are the marks of Methodism today? Compare your view with the extract in Box 7.
2. John Wesley based his doctrine on scripture, tradition, reason and experience. Which do you think the most important and why?
3. How would you explain to a non-Christian what John Wesley meant by 'grace'? How important is grace to you?
4. There were certain 'ideas in the air', arising from the Enlightenment, to which John Wesley reacted both positively and negatively. What ideas, to which we must respond, are 'in the air' for us?
5. 'Wesley's understanding of the church came from participation in the life of the church.' Does your participation lead you to similar or very different views of the church? Do we take Wesley's ideas sufficiently seriously?

2

After Wesley

Wesley's legacy

John Wesley created a theological atmosphere but he did not bequeath a definitive theological system to his successors. His Conferences were times for theological discussion but the conversations were ongoing and never concluded.

It is appropriate, therefore, to ask: how is a theological tradition to be identified? What evidence does it leave to enable us to reconstruct its development? Do we turn primarily to published books or to people who are understood to be 'theologians'? Or should we also refer to sermons, popular journals and incidental writings? This is an especially important question in the case of a tradition which understands itself to be practical and does not place a premium on formal, systematic theological treatises.

Methodism in the first half of the nineteenth century had a life of its own but breathed a common evangelical atmosphere and was motivated by its mission. Its members, sharing in a relatively stable, self-conscious British culture, were aware of social status and lived with its limitations and possibilities. Much attention was focussed inwards, questions of church order being paramount and often contentious. As a result, there was debate – and then secessions, new configurations and fresh momentum. The outcome, theologically speaking [16], was that Wesleyan Methodist polity and mission combined to shape distinctive emphases within a self-contained community.

16. Wesleyan Methodism throughout my childhood and youth was almost entirely self-enclosed so far as its theological outlook was concerned. Wesley's Sermons and *Notes on the New Testament* constituted its standards of Christian doctrine. Special prominence was given to what John Wesley had termed 'our doctrines', namely, Universal Redemption through Christ, as against Calvinism, Justification by Faith, New Birth through the Spirit, the Direct Witness of the Holy Spirit, giving full assurance of acceptance with God and adoption as His sons, with the doctrine of entire sanctification as 'perfect love'.

Source: John Scott Lidgett, *My Guided Life*, Methuen 1936, p. 144.

Media of theological tradition

Some books were especially important. Richard Watson's *Theological Institutes* became required reading for many Methodist ministers in Great Britain and North America, and the influence of books continued in the late nineteenth century with W. B. Pope's *A Compendium of Christian Theology*. Even so, much of the Methodist theological tradition was carried by other media, especially sermons and the magazines which commanded general attention. *The Arminian Magazine*, for example, founded by Wesley in 1778 and later called *The Methodist Magazine*, contained theological discussions, biographical materials, letters and, by the second year, poetry.

The role of Wesley's sermons

Illustrative of a remarkable openness was the role of Wesley's sermons in the theological instruction of Methodists. Richard P. Heitzenrater attempts a clarification of an exceedingly complicated process:

In the late 1740s Wesley began to draw up model deeds upon which to fix his preaching houses; . . . In the Model Deed printed in the 'Large Minutes' of 1763, the trustees of the preaching houses are given explicit authority not only to see that only those preachers appointed by Mr Wesley were to preach there, but also as the Deed states, to see 'that such persons preach no other Doctrine than is contained in *Mr Wesley's Notes upon the New Testament*, and four volumes of Sermons'. The wording again is important: the Methodist preachers (unlicensed to be sure, and mostly uneducated) were required to preach 'no other doctrine' than that contained in the *Sermons* and *Notes*. These two documents then acted as *boundaries* not patterns; they provided the limits beyond which the Methodist preachers were not to preach. Wesley was using the *Sermons* with regard to his preachers in a similar fashion to the way the Church of England used the Homilies with regard to its unlicensed and uneducated preachers. The intention was to guarantee, as far as possible, sound doctrine, to be sure. But we should point out that his purpose was different from the Church's – he was more interested in *edification* that would promote *holiness* of life than in *enforcement* that would simply guarantee *uniformity* of doctrine.[1]

Heitzenrater draws a sharp contrast. There was ambiguity, however – and tension, a tension which resists neat demarcation, so that both boundary and pattern were present together.

But now a problem arose: which of the sermons were taken to have authority? Again Heitzenrater unfolds the story:[2]

Only as British Methodism entered the 1830s did it begin to look like a church. And, interestingly enough, at that precise time the wording of the model Deed regarding the *Sermons* and *Notes* was changed. Where it had said the preachers must 'preach *no other doctrine than* is contained in Notes . . . and in the first four volumes of Sermons'. It was then changed to read 'No person . . . shall be permitted to preach . . . who shall maintain, promulgate, or teach any doctrine or practice, *contrary to what is contained in Notes on the New Testament* . . . and in the first four volumes of Sermons . . .' [. . .] The shift, one might say, represents a move from using the Wesleyan documents as *boundaries* to using the *Sermons* and *Notes* as *patterns* . . . Methodism in Great Britain was beginning in some ways to see itself as a church with a qualified (as well as called) ministry . . . In 1763 that would have meant the forty-three sermons in the original four volumes (or forty-four sermons, if you include the sermon 'Wandering Thoughts', added in a second edition of volume three published also sometime in 1763). But in 1771–72, Wesley began the publication of his collected works with the four volumes of *Sermons on Several Occasions*. In this edition, however, he included nine additional sermons that he had written in the 1760s, after the appearance of the original fourth volume. '*The four volumes* of Wesley's Sermons' in the *Works* thus contained fifty-three sermons. The picture becomes even more complicated in the 1780s when Wesley decided to publish a new collection of sermons that would include those additional sermons he had written for publication in *The Arminian Magazine* during the previous decade. This third collection (eight volumes) includes a republication of the previous four volumes plus four new volumes plus the extra one from a later edition of volume three, making forty-four sermons in these 'four volumes . . .'

Jackson, when he published Wesley's *Works* in the 1820s and 30s, simply stated that this phrase referred to the first four volumes of the *Works* published in the 1770s (53 minus the one on the death of Whitefield equals 52). But persistent questions during the rest of the nineteenth century eventually forced the matter into the hands of Chancery Lane lawyers, who in 1914 finally decided (for better or worse) that 'the first four volumes' specified in the Model Deed were in fact volumes 1–4 in the edition of 1787–88 and included forty-four sermons.[3]

The difficulty in ascertaining Wesley's exact sermonic bequest points to the difficulty of preserving or presenting a complete statement of doctrine [17].

---

17. . . . repentance towards God; a present, free, and full salvation from sin; – a salvation flowing from the grace of God alone 'through the redemption that is in Christ Jesus', and apprehended by the simple exercise of faith; – a salvation which begins with the forgiveness of sins (this forgiveness being certified to the penitent believer by the Holy Spirit) and (by means of this witness, but by the power of that Divine Spirit who bears the witness) a change of heart; – a salvation which is itself the only entrance to a course of practical holiness.

Source: 1820 Wesleyan Conference, Resolution on the 'Leading and Vital Doctrines of the Gospel'.

The crucial issue

Methodism had received an initial theological impetus, and Wesley, in pointing to a distinctive style of doing theology, did intend to present essential Christian doctrines. But the theological path which he attempted to chart was as difficult as it was different. As we have seen, to emphasize properly the relation between free grace and free will proved elusive, and followers often lost the way or altered the balance. Opponents to the Wesleyan synthesis came from both sides, some wanting to stress exclusively God's action, others wanting to give greater weight to human action. Wesley's way was to begin with and emphasize God's grace while also honouring the integrity of responsive

agents. But this balance proved fragile and, despite John Fletcher's important contribution, succeeding generations of interpreters witness to the difficulty of preserving it. As a result [18], efforts to restrict or close the system increased.

---

18. In spite of his political Toryism, Wesley had been a man of large sympathies, quick to seize opportunities presented by new situations and to appreciate the bearing of the Gospel upon them. The Wesleyanism of the generation after his death was no longer a new and still elastic creation but an organism with a tradition to be guarded.

Source: N. P. Goldhawk, 'Early Victorian Age: Spirituality and Worship' in Rupert Davies and Gordon Rupp (eds), *A History of The Methodist Church in Great Britain*, Vol. I, Epworth Press 1978, p. 118.

Two figures stand out as most important among the early successors to Wesley, Adam Clarke and Richard Watson. Clarke was primarily a biblical scholar, while Watson was a systematic theologian and the chief theological spokesman for nineteenth century British Methodism in the transition from Wesley.

Adam Clarke

It is appropriate to begin with Adam Clarke (1760?–1832). He was in every way a remarkable man, exceedingly intelligent, religiously intense and always serious. To speak of him as a hard worker is to grossly understate the case. Self-educated and prodigiously educated, he was vigorously disciplined in all things and became one of the leading linguists of his time. Thus he translated the New Testament, wrote a commentary on the entire Bible and, as archivist for the British Museum, translated the Coptic on the Rosetta Stone. As a preacher – he began preaching at eighteen years of age and continued to his death – he wrote and delivered sermons that were meticulously prepared, and published. He was President of the Methodist Conference in England on three occasions and in Ireland four times, and he engaged in both intellectual and social issues of his time.

Autobiography

Clarke was aware of his achievement and, in his autobiography, states his reasons for recounting his life:

> To exhibit a man through every period of his life, who has obtained some distinction as well in the republic of letters as in religious society [is valuable]:
>
> 1. To manifest the good grace of God to those who trust in him; . . . 2ndly. To prevent the publication of improper accounts . . .; 3rdly, To show to young men who have not had those advantages which arise from elevated birth and a liberal education how such defects may be supplied by persevering industry, and the redemption of time.[4]

All of this he embodied; what he commends he himself achieved. His autobiography is honest and modest and persistently extols the grace of God. Though it presumes his own importance and substantial contributions, it would be taken, if written by a biographer, as a direct and unexaggerated account.

Adam Clarke overlapped with John Wesley whom he knew, by whom he was commissioned, and whose life and message he greatly respected. He claims that he had come to his theological positions [19] on his own and was both surprised and pleased to discover that his basic convictions were entirely congruent with Methodist beliefs.[5]

---

19. As eternal life is given IN the Son of God, it follows it cannot be enjoyed WITHOUT him. No man can have it without having Christ, therefore 'he that hath the Son hath life', and 'he that hath not the Son hath not life'. It is in vain to expect eternal glory if we have not Christ in our heart. The indwelling Christ gives both a title to it and a meetness for it. This is God's record. Let no man deceive himself here. An indwelling Christ, and glory; no indwelling Christ, no glory. God's record must stand.

Source: Adam Clarke, 'Justification' from *Christian Theology*, London 1835, pp. 158–89.

Core convictions

He also taught through sermons, carefully prepared and with a sharp focus. In his sermon xxiii, 'Love to God and Man: The Fulfilling of the Law and the Prophets', Matt. 22.35–40, he summarizes his core convictions:

> The Christian *religion* is a revelation from God himself, giving a knowledge of His own being, attributes, and works: and of *man*, his nature, present state, and necessities; shewing also the *way* in which the whole human race may have all their spiritual wants supplied, their souls delivered from evil passions, and be made partakers of a divine nature, escape the corruption that is in the world, through evil desire, and being made truly holy, become in consequence contented and happy, and stand in a continual preparation for blessedness of the eternal world.[6]

In such a position the Holy Spirit occupies a central place [20], and one of the best extended developments of these central themes is found in the last sermon in his collection, xxxviii, 'Apostolic Preaching'.[7] In his text, Col. 1.27–8, he finds these chief points.

I. What was the *sum and substance* of the Apostle's preaching – 'Christ in you the hope of glory'.
II. What was the *manner* and *way* in which he preached – 'warning every man and teaching every man in all wisdom'.
III. What was the *end* for which he preached – 'That he might present every man perfect in Christ Jesus'.[8]

---

20. The Holy Spirit in the soul of a believer is God's seal, set on his heart to testify that he is God's property, and that he should be wholly employed in God's service.

As Christ is represented as the ambassador of the Father, so the Holy Spirit is represented as the ambassador of the Son, coming vested with his authority, as the interpreter and executor of His will.

Source: Adam Clarke, 'The Holy Spirit' from *Christian Theology*, London 1835, p. 176.

Significance

In Adam Clarke we find a true successor of John Wesley. The two were alike not only in character and religious seriousness but in the content and modes of their theological reflection. Both were first of all preachers, both understood theology as undergirding Christian proclamation and Christian living, both were thoroughly engaged in all aspects of the Methodist movement, and both understood theological instruction as nurturing Christian life into Christian holiness.

Richard Watson

Richard Watson (1781–1833) was the next major theological influence in early nineteenth-century Methodism. He was also a remarkable man who developed his native intelligence to an extremely high degree. Self-educated, he edited a dictionary of biblical and theological topics and in his major work, *Theological Institutes*, displayed extensive knowledge of historical and contemporary theological discussion.

Both Clarke and Watson exhibited how fundamental Christian commitment can lead to extraordinary achievement. Yet, as we shall see, they develop their theologies in very different ways: Clarke continued Wesley's theological understanding and style; Watson changed both but, even so, became the dominant influence in Methodist theology for the first half of the nineteenth century.[9]

Deviation from Wesley's method

In spirit, style and substance Watson was radically different from John Wesley, though his concentration on the central role of salvation and his essentially 'Arminian Wesleyan' interpretations retain a family resemblance [21]. Indeed, the resemblance was so strong that his role as theological spokesman for Methodism was neither doubted nor challenged, and his book became the chief theological text for the education of Methodist ministers both in Great Britain and North America.

---

21. It is allowed, and all scriptural advocates of the universal redemption of mankind will join with the Calvinists in maintaining the doctrine, that every disposition and inclination to good which originally existed in the nature of man is lost by the fall . . . But as all men are required to do those things which have a saving tendency, we contend that the grace to them has been bestowed upon all. Equally sacred is the doctrine to be held, that no person can repent or truly believe except under the influence of the Spirit of God; and that we have no ground of boasting, in ourselves, but that all the glory of our salvation, commenced and consummated, is to be given to God alone, as the result of the freeness and riches of his grace . . .

These premises, also, secure the glory of our salvation to the grace of God . . . by showing that his [human] agency even when rightly directed, is upheld and influenced by the superior power of God, and yet so as to be still his own.

Source: Richard Watson, *Theological Institutes*, IV, 132.

To claim that Watson was different from Wesley in these ways runs counter to dominant interpretations of their relationship. E. Dale Dunlap, who has done extensive work on nineteenth-century British Methodist theology, states the usual evaluation, namely, that Watson was not an innovator but rather intended to follow the principles inherent in John Wesley's work.[10] He further states that 'The forty years following the death of John Wesley saw no radical change in the theological fabric of Methodism. Mr Wesley's successors were motivated, as he was, by an evangelistic zeal for the salvation of men's souls so that they relegated the concerns for doctrinal elaboration to a second but not unimportant position.'[11]

But this interpretation seems inadequate. There is no doubt that Richard Watson was motivated by a driving evangelistic passion and a missionary zeal, and in this he continued John Wesley's primary commitment. It may also be the case that Watson relegated doctrinal concern to a secondary place in his basic order of priority. Moreover, his effort to write an accurate biography of John Wesley and his proposed biography of Charles Wesley are clear evidence of his alliance to the Methodist movement and its leaders. Nonetheless, when Watson turns to theology he contructs a system which is isolated from his evangelistic, missionary impulse; that is, he deals with theology as an intellectual enterprise and one which serves to answer intellectual questions. In his understanding, theology serves preaching at a distance in that it provides intellectual support for the doctrines preached and helps clear the ground from intellectual encumbrances which might prevent or distort belief. Theology, for Watson, is a theoretical, even a catechetical, enterprise.

John Wesley, if our assessment of him in the previous chapter was correct, was not principally concerned with either systematic theology or apologetics. But these are precisely Watson's interests and provide the dominant characteristics of his *Theological Institutes*.

This matter of theological character is subtle. It is clear that Watson understood himself as a disciple of John Wesley continuing the Wesleyan mission, and much of what he did was expressive of this spirit. But there is a decisive break when he falls back upon more traditional modes of theological construction – found in Protestant and Roman Catholic traditions that were more systematic than was typical of the Anglican tradition – and develops a theological system which was deduced from a scriptural base and addressed to a theological/intellectual audience. In this he deviated from John Wesley's innovative work in practical theology. Oddly, Richard Watson followed Wesley more closely in all other things than he did as a theologian. As a result, well-deserved respect for his leadership in Connexional affairs gave him the influence to direct Methodist theology down a path which deviated from Wesley's distinctive effort.

Structure of the *Theological Institutes*

Watson's constructive theology constituted a reordering of the approach and the role of theology in Methodism. The structure of *Theological Institutes* sets the character of his work. The presentation is apologetic and intends to address the doubts and answer the objections of opponents ranging from unbelievers to believers with different theological points of view. Consequently, he understands theology as answering questions raised by intellectuals and as dealing with issues discussed among intellectuals.

The two fundamental principles upon which he builds are the authority and complete adequacy of scripture and the moral agency or freedom of human beings and, therefore, their ability to receive scriptural revelation [22]. His manner of treating these two themes is to answer questions raised by philosophers and theologians, and in doing so he sets a trend in Methodist doctrinal construction. From the beginning there had been emphasis on the primacy of preaching to the masses of people and the effort of theology was to undergird the presentation of Christian truth. With Wesley and Clarke, therefore, the primary concentration was on clarification of the gospel message. But with Watson the focus shifted to a concentration on the intellectual context in which the gospel was

---

22. The theological system of the holy Scriptures being the subject of our inquiries, it is essential to our undertaking to establish their divine authority. But before the direct evidence which the case admits is adduced, our attention may be profitably engaged by several considerations which afford presumptive evidence in favour of the revelations of the Old and New Testaments. These are of so much weight that they ought not, in fairness, to be overlooked; nor can their force be easily resisted by the impartial inquirer.

The moral agency of man is a principle on which much depends in such an investigation, and, from its bearing upon the question at issue requires our first notice.

He is a moral agent who is capable of performing moral actions; and an action is rendered moral for two circumstances – that it is voluntary and that is has respect to some rule which determines it to be good or evil. 'Moral good or evil', says Locke, 'is the conformity or disagreement of our voluntary actions to some law, whereby good or evil is drawn upon us from the will or power of the law-maker.'

Source: Richard Watson, *Theological Institutes*, I, 1.

preached and heard. So important is this approach for Watson that he spends the entire first part of his *Institutes*, some 260 pages, exploring and arguing the themes of scriptural authority and human agency before he turns to the theological content which, granted these assumptions, can be formulated.

The theological system of the Holy Scriptures

Scripture is always – consistently and thoroughly – the primary point of reference in Watson's theology; his intention is to present 'The theological system of the Holy Scriptures'. Establishing the scriptural base is of primary importance for it represents Watson's move from Wesley's more dynamic and open theological enterprise to establishing the primacy of scripture and then deducing theological conclusions from it. The extended discussion of scripture as the foundation of his system represents a shift from the free grace of God expressed in Jesus Christ as communicated through the Holy Spirit to an emphasis upon a commanding text which controls experience. Hence, God's creative interaction with human beings is replaced by textual control.

This issue is significant and requires sensitive statement. Wesley always respects the authority of scripture and his sermons were often strings of biblical quotations. But for Wesley it was not the text of scripture, *per se*, which conveyed truth. Rather the Holy Spirit enlivened scripture to become God's word, which evoked faith and led to discipleship. Christian truth, therefore, is found through the experience of Jesus Christ as enlivened by the Holy Spirit and as confirmed in transformed life, and scripture bears witness to this possibility. Richard Watson, by contrast, took over Wesley's seriousness about the Bible, placed scripture at the beginning of his system, and then used it to frame what was discussed. In this process attention shifts from God's immediate, initiating agency to the biblical text. Scripture, for Wesley, is always kept in tension with and is interpreted through tradition, reason and experience. For Watson, who assumed that scripture is consistent and non-historically formed, proposi-

tions built upon proof texts prescribed the formation of Christian doctrine.

Nevertheless, to gain a complete picture of Watson's effort, it is necessary to point out that, while he shifted the base and framework, he kept much of the content of Wesley's theology. Evidently this achievement depended on an unrecognized split between, on the one hand, his experience and what he had learned from Wesley and, on the other, his borrowing from other theological traditions to construct his systematic statement. For him the two lived together [23], but he bequeathed a structure which would make it difficult for successors to continue the more authentic and dynamic Wesleyan emphases.

23. The doctrines of justification by faith, the assurance of pardon, regeneration, and divine influence which had been considered by many as necessarily connected with the Calvinistic scheme, were now seen in harmony with the doctrines of God's universal love, the unrestricted extent of Christ's death, and the fulness of divine grace. Men were not compelled into a choice between two extremes, Calvinism and Pelagianism, into which last error most of our English divines had fallen in opposing the doctrine of decrees.

Source: Richard Watson, *Observations on Southey's Life of Wesley*, pp. 132–33.

The moral agency of human beings is essential to Watson's argument and follows immediately upon the establishment of an inerrant scriptural base. Revelation must be received, not simply enforced; salvation offered in Jesus Christ is for all people, and everyone is morally responsible for accepting or rejecting God's offer of salvation. This theme is Wesleyan and undergirds the necessity of preaching and calling for conversion. It is of importance, however, that in his *Theological Institutes* Watson develops only modestly the theme of holiness, his attention being focussed on the capacity for reception of salvation through justification and regeneration. He accepts holiness but does not add significantly to the doctrine.

Doctrines of the Holy Scriptures

After establishing his foundation, Watson presents 'Doctrines of the Holy Scriptures', namely, the doctrines of God, Jesus Christ and the Holy Spirit. The doctrine of God is central (9 chapters), the doctrine of Jesus Christ concentrates on his divinity (6 chapters, 1 chapter on his humanity), and the doctrine of the Holy Spirit is given one chapter. The character of the triune persons is central to this section, which is followed by a treatment of the doctrines of human fall and redemption.

Watson has a strong sense of human sin and, on this subject, quotes Wesley and Jonathan Edwards as equal authorities.[12] He also quotes Wesley as an authoritative example of an Arminian who 'earnestly' and 'vigorously' supports justification by faith[13] and places much emphasis on God's gracious action, centered in the work of Jesus Christ.

The *Theological Institutes* are completed (Part III) with a discussion of 'The Morals of Christianity' (4 chapters) and (Part IV) the 'Institutions of Christianity' which is a discussion of church order and sacraments (3 chapters). The number of chapters gives some indication of the amount of attention given to each topic. The treatment of the themes is consistent with Wesley's position but does not fully represent his distinctive perspective.

Implications for Methodist self-understanding

What does such a change in style and spirit indicate for Methodist self-understanding? It means that engagement with theological issues is separated from actual practice. Unlike Wesley, who by keeping theory and practice in tight interaction had explored new terrain, Watson concentrates upon theory and intellectual justification. In other words, as he develops his independent theoretical statement, he casts many of Wesley's theological emphases in a form which, though traditional, is in fact alien to them. The implication of this is that Methodist theology becomes one step removed from the actual practice of Christian preaching and Christian living.

In serving the evangelistic mission of preaching the gospel, Watson increasingly concentrates on the context in which the gospel is preached and heard. There continues to be concern for the character of the gospel, such as its universal call to faith and its proclamation of the triune God, the divinity of Jesus Christ and the person of the Holy Spirit. But even these emphases are dealt with by answering objections to them and by providing them with rational support.

It is especially significant, moreover, that Watson developed his notion of human freedom without firmly and thoroughly rooting it in prevenient grace as given in Jesus Christ. Regarded as a whole, in fact, Watson's *Theological Institutes* offer little explicit concentration on distinctive Methodist doctrines such as prevenient grace or sanctification. As a result, Watson establishes a direction which moves away from John Wesley's distinctive mode of practical theology. Watson's audience is the intellectually able and concerned, and he wants to answer other theologians rather than make sure that the message conveyed is understandable for ordinary listeners. It is important that Wesley used sermons to convey his interpretation of Christian faith. In contrast, Watson uses theological treatises which set the context for preaching more than the content of preaching.

With Richard Watson, Methodist theology establishes a family likeness with more traditional Protestant and Roman Catholic theological styles and loses its special, Wesleyan character. Because of the repeated Arminian emphases, the stress on scriptural authority and the central concern with human salvation, there remains continuity with John Wesley; but a different understanding of the source and style of theology is endorsed by those for whom Richard Watson is the theological spokesman.

But the Methodist tradition took more than one form, and in the nineteenth century several found sharp expression. Robert Currie comments on the nineteenth century: 'The division of Methodism was a small reformation. Theological, social and organizational conflicts created, on the one side the Wesleyan Methodist Connexion, a massive ecclesiastical organization which friend and foe, Protestant and Catholic alike, have often compared to Roman Catholicism; and on the other, a dozen or more denominations more or less in opposition to Wesleyanism. Wesleyan catholicity – its doctrines of ministry and sacrament, its stress on order, its hierarchical rule – suggest many Roman analogies, reformed Methodism's doctrine of spiritual equality, its stress on evangelism, its system of representative government, have obvious parallels in Protestantism as a whole. The two cardinal ideas of the Reformation, justification by faith and the priesthood of all believers, could find far more unqualified acceptance in reformed Methodism than among Wesleyans.'[14]

William Arthur

In mid-century and for the next several decades, there was an atypical but popular voice among Methodists – that of William Arthur (1819–1901). An Irishman, who decided early to become a Methodist minister, Arthur was educated in a classical school and in the Wesleyan Theological Institute in London. He went to India as a missionary, then served Methodist churches in Paris and Boulogne. When he returned to England and Ireland he served as a circuit minister, as a leader in the Missionary Society and as Principal of the Methodist College in Belfast. He was renowned as a powerful speaker and preacher in Great Britain and in the United States [24], and his writing was a continuation of his preaching ministry.

---

24. Behold Him, how much he sacrifices and how much he endures! behold the unspeakable glory which follows this sacrifice; and ask him to make us to taste the fellowship of his sufferings, to put that mind in us which was also in him. Wait, ponder, contemplate, pray, and stay long by that cross rather than go unblest. He will breathe his mind into your mind, he will form his character in your heart, he will possess you with his own spirit, and move you with his motives, till your natural impulses are vanquished by impulses from him, and your soul will be a new creature, like Jesus, loving as he also loved.

Source: William Arthur, 'Christ Saving Others and Sacrificing Himself' in *Addresses*, New York 1858, p. 129.

Teaching about holiness

Perhaps his most influential book was *The Tongue of Fire*, first published in 1856. The book, going through eighteen printings within three years, became a powerful impetus for the renewal of interest in Christian holiness on both sides of the Atlantic. It did not so much extend understanding of sanctification as persuasively call for recognition of this dimension of experience and for participation in it.

Defence of the Christian world-view

But Arthur was also a Christian apologist. In a series of books he addresses several pressing theological issues. He is especially concerned about the relation of religion to science, and he challenges the views of Augustus Comte [25] and John Stuart Mill. These two philosophers, he argues, hold that there is one set of laws which govern all things. In contrast, Arthur holds that there are two laws: one moral, one physical. The first set of laws are those which allow free moral agency; the second set act necessarily.

With sustained eloquence, he carefully defines terms and distinguishes nine orders of relationships, from relations of unconscious entities to relations of reciprocal action and moral obligation to one another, to a common external authority and to a Higher Power.[15] The relations between unconscious agents are fixed and inviolable. The relations of moral agents are also fixed but *not* as unavoidable; the difference is the freedom of conscious agents. With this move,

---

25. When the Republic of 1848 was in power, Comte published his 'Discours sur l'Ensemble du Positivisme', and set upon the title-page the motto: *To reorganize [society] without God or king, by the systematic worship of humanity*. The moral purpose of the whole school of the positivists was never better expressed. It was not so much the king from whom 'emancipation' was desired as the King of kings.

Source: William Arthur, *On the Difference between Physical and Moral Law*, London 1883, p. 218.

Arthur intended to secure the base of Christian morality and worship.

He continued his argument against current assumptions, cleverly contrasting *God Without Religion* (1886), in which he challenges the popular deistic position of Fitzjames Stephen, and *Religion Without God* (1888), in which he challenges the positivism of Frederick Harrison and the agnosticism of Herbert Spencer. These books constitute a substantial apologetic effort to counter anti-Christian philosophies and to present a Christian interpretation of the natural and social worlds. Arthur has a capacity for sustained thought, for focussing on essential issues, and for sharp rhetorical commentary; and he was exploring these subjects of contemporary intellectual importance at a time when most of his Methodist contemporaries were satisfied to repeat inherited theological formulae and to remain within the believing community.

It is significant that Arthur was also a promoter of 'The Ladies' Committee for the Amelioration of the Condition of Women in Heathen Countries'. Consistently he expresses an ethical impulse.

Role as a Christian philosopher

William Arthur represents a change from the theological effort of Richard Watson. Arthur takes on philosophical issues of his day, very much accepting the field of debate as established by philosophers. He argues with them on their own terrain and makes counter points which are more congenial to a theological understanding of nature, the human condition and the possibility of affirming the reality of God.

Arthur does not begin with a scripture base or argue deductively from scripture. Rather, he functions as a Christian philosopher who accepts a challenge that has been offered and responds with vigour. Large intellectual issues of his day are tackled as he attempts to provide a basis upon which Christian affirmations may be reasonably expressed. His arguments stand or fall according to their ability to be rationally convincing.

In the interplay of theory and practice, Arthur weights his theological attention on the side of theory. There is for him, however, an interaction, for his concern with philosophical issues arises from his preaching and he recognizes the interdependence of theology and ethics. The two are held together as an expression of his total ministry and of his inherited sense of theology serving effective proclamation. In all of this Arthur exhibits what will, several generations later, become typical of British Methodist theology. In the meantime, the dominant influence of Richard Watson continues, particularly as he set the background for the work of William Burt Pope.

A Time of Culmination

The second half of the nineteenth century was Queen Victoria's era, that distinctive time designated as the Victorian Age. It was the time of the dominance of the British Empire. Britannia ruled the waves, and the empire's financial growth and world influence were monumental. Obviously Methodism shared in the social and economic benefits which the global empire brought. Even so, most Methodists – Arthur was an exception – lived in isolation from many of the intellectual influences which shaped the era. Darwin's ideas were not taken into consideration by Methodist theologians; idealism in philosophy made no impact; the struggle with religious doubt and the relation of faith to ethics did not impinge in any significant way; and the new interest in world religions was not acknowledged or made a part of their intellectual consideration.

Socially, economically and politically the Methodist movement, for most of the nineteenth century, accepted its existing context. Its primary concern was focussed on redemption of life and the fulfilment of individual, personal experience within this structure. Relatively little notice was taken of cultural conditions or of developments in both the pre-Victorian and the Victorian eras. The rise of secularism (defined by G. J. Holyoake as the improvement of life by material means, belief in science as the available providence, the freeing of morality from religious bases, and the intellectual issues of evolution and Idealistic philosophy) and changes in educational curricula were all of little importance. Methodism, in short, was carried along by the general economic, political and social conditions, but for the most part it lived within its own confines [26] and the daily challenge of living was dealt with in terms of finding, developing and sharing a fulfilling Christian existence. Theologically, this meant that Methodist intellectual leaders spoke from within the believing community and to this community. The major concern was to interpret faith for believers and to preserve the distinctiveness of Methodist thought and action.

---

26. The chapel gave them their first music, their first literature and philosophy to meet the harsh life and cruel impact of the crude materialistic age. Here men first found the language and art to express their antagonism to grim conditions and injustice.

Source: Lord Lawson, *A Man's Life*, Hodder and Stoughton 1944, p. 69.

There was one notable exception to Methodists refraining from political involvement. The 1830 Wesleyan Conference, with the leadership of Richard Watson, urged members to use their votes to bring the system of slavery to an end.

In the last two decades of the nineteenth century, however, Methodism was drawn into the general swirl of social change in the life of the nation. This was due in part to the growth of Nonconformist church membership among the general populace, in part to a new awareness of its own contribution and challenge to British life, and in part to the pressure of general intellectual issues which demanded attention, especially the issues of biblical criticism, of human status in the natural and social orders and the meaning of the atonement. The persistent question was: what are the essential elements of Christian faith? The two major figures, who led the confronting of these issues, were Hugh Price Hughes in the social arena and John Scott Lidgett in the intellectual arena (see chapter 4).

Various Methodist groups had shaped the tradition as it moved through the second half of the nineteenth century. That there was an interweaving of the various strands of the Methodist movement is no surprise, for all traditions are complex.[16] Yet we must be careful not to take generalizations as exact representations. Maldwyn Edwards, for example, is able in *After Wesley* to discuss 'The Dominant Toryism of [Wesleyan] Methodism', documenting relevant attitudes, at least through the first half of the nineteenth century. But he can also indicate the contemporaneous 'Underlying Liberalism' which was pressing for very different attitudes within the church. Over time, political affiliations did change and, while the allegiances of Wesleyan Methodists certainly shifted [27], this was also true of the entire Methodist movement. Both continuity and change were present and struggled with one another.

---

27. After 1850 Wesleyan Methodism could no longer be described as Tory in politics and closely attached to the Church [of England]. Finding its strength drawn almost wholly from the commercial and industrial classes it had become increasingly Nonconformist in its sympathies, and Radical in its outlook. The old connection with the Church was almost forgotten. The final revolt against [Jabez] Bunting and his friends was more than a personal animus. It was a new attitude to politics and social reform. If Liberalism in the second half of the nineteenth century owed much to Nonconformist support, it was because Nonconformity has been reinforced by a new and powerful ally. In the middle period of Methodism the dominating figure was Jabez Bunting, the Tory. In the last period of Methodism the dominating figure was Hugh Price Hughes, the Radical.

Source: Maldwyn Edwards, *After Wesley*, Epworth Press 1935, p. 161.

William Burt Pope

William Burt Pope represented the fullest flowering of the theological tradition which began with Richard Watson and which basically characterized British Methodism through the middle quarters of the nineteenth century. In Pope was found the highest achievement of Methodist self-consciousness combined with a generous attitude towards other Christian traditions. He was inclusively 'catholic' in his sympathies: willing to recognize indebtedness to others, while also maintaining his proud and distinctive inheritance from John Wesley and his followers.

The 'eclecticism' of Methodist theology

A central theme in his description of Methodist theology was that it was 'eclectic,' [28] – in other words, it acknowledged its wide indebtedness, especially to the undivided early church (explicitly the Apostles, the Nicene and the Athanasian Creeds), the Protestant reformers and the Church of England. Together with mysticism, which Pope recognized as specially influential upon himself, all of these contributions converged in a rich amalgam in the work of John Wesley and his followers. For Wesley's theology had drawn elements from all of these traditions, had reshaped them and forged an evangelical theology which focussed upon human salvation, both in its

---

28. The defenders of Methodist theology . . . claim to hold all essential truth; to omit no articles but those which they consider erroneous; and to disparage none but those which they deem unessential. This, of course, is a high pretention, but it is not a vainglorious one; for surely it is the prerogative of every Christian community to glory in holding 'the faith once delivered to the saints'. And as it is with the doctrines, so it is with the spirit of Methodist teaching. In this also it is, after a fashion, eclectic, as it sympathizes with those who make it their boast that they know no other theology than the biblical, and is as biblical as they. It also agrees with those who think that divinity is a systematic science, to be grounded and organized as such, while with almost all its heart it joins the company of Mystics, whose supreme theologian is the interior Teacher, and who find all truth in the experimental vision and knowledge of God in Christ.

Source: William Burt Pope, 'Methodist Doctrine', *The Wesley Memorial Volume* ed J. O. A. Clark, New York 1880, p. 182.

---

initial stages of justification and reconciliation and in its mature development in Christian holiness.

Pope's own scholarly credentials were impressive. He was a thorough student of the biblical and classical languages, read widely in British and German literature, was disciplined in his thought and achieved a remarkable clarity and succinctness in his theological writing. Descriptions of his character reflect the integrity of his life and thought: he exhibited what he expressed; he was committed, careful and humble.

Limitations of a self-restricted tradition

At the same time, Pope represented the limitations of a self-restricted tradition, one which stayed within its own confines and did not seek interaction with other contemporary intellectual movements. Hence, while he was thoroughly trained in biblical languages, he had little interest in the contemporary work of establishing the best biblical text for study (which was becoming prominent in the work of F. J. A. Hort and B. F. Westcott in Great Britain); and he was hostile to critical biblical work which was common in Germany. Pope's own position was that the scriptural text as it had been generally transmitted was accurate, authoritative and sufficient and that the work of biblical scholarship was to provide expositions of that received text.

He was indifferent to current work in philosophy and hostile to the scientific developments of his day. At no point does he engage with the philosophical discussions of British Idealism which had become prominent with Thomas H. Green in the 1860s and which grew to dominate university intellectual life by late in the century. He dismisses Charles Darwin's scientific work and does not participate in the discussions of encroaching secularism or the relation of Christian faith to the social order. Pope was a tower of strength within an enclosed tradition. He gave impressive expression to the themes which had formed Methodist theology, but his statement was a restatement; it did not bring these themes into engagement with current issues, questions or challenges.

There was one development where awareness of

surrounding issues may have influenced him. Pope makes a distinction between natural theology, that is the minimum theology which all people may articulate on the basis of their native ability and capacity for rational thought, and special revelation manifest in Jesus Christ. While such a distinction may have been an implication in Watson's discussion of the moral agency of human beings, it was becoming prominent in the last decades of the nineteenth century as was especially evident in Lord Adam Gifford's endowment for lectures in natural theology in the Scottish universities and was becoming prominent in the study of the history of religions, especially non-Western and non-Christian religions. Pope, without extensive discussion, makes room for natural theology, but he maintains that the God who is meagerly known in common human experience is decisively and fully known in the special revelation in Jesus Christ.

The centrality of Jesus Christ

The centrality of Jesus Christ is the heart of Pope's theology. He sets this doctrine within a general framework which includes the reality of God as the source, subject and end of theology. As source, God takes the initiative to make God's self known through revelation and a part of this revelation can be known to sensitive, rational persons. This implies an ability to appreciate and receive revelation, so that communication between God and human beings is possible; but this revelation is brought to its climax in the person of Jesus Christ who clarifies revelation and enlivens its reception. This is the base of Christian theology, namely, the focus on Jesus Christ. This entire account is present in scripture, which provides the content of theology. But the scriptural themes need to be systematized, and Pope understands his task to be that of supplying such a systematic statement of Christian truth.

Dialogue with other Christian traditions

True to his catholic spirit, Pope was in conversation with the full range of people and traditions which had influenced Methodist theology. He was fundamentally positive in his appreciation of many contributions made by other Christian traditions and tended to stress points of agreement. But he continued the long debate with Calvinism over the issue of the 'covenant of grace' and the 'covenant of works'. With Wesley, he wants to hold faith and works together: grace as received and expressed cannot be separated, justification and sanctification are both to be included under the gracious relations of God to human beings.

Methodist Arminianism

With Arminian emphasis and in keeping with the articles of the English church, he maintains that persons are 'far gone' from original righteousness and of their own nature are inclined to sin and that there is hope only in God's gracious forgiveness and renewal of life. Hence, there is a strong Wesleyan emphasis upon the enabling grace, prevenient grace, which comes through the redemption of Jesus Christ. He is also clear that Christian holiness is a revered and distinctive Methodist doctrine and should be emphasized [29]. Once, again, the themes of human salvation and the role of Jesus Christ in that salvation are central. On this basis, he claims that Methodist theology consistently and fully connected the universality of grace with possible universality of redemption. Grace, through Jesus Christ, was free for all and to all people.

---

29. It cannot be too distinctly impressed that the one element in Methodist doctrine that may be called distinctive, is the article that the work of the Spirit in sanctifying believers from sin – from all that in the divine estimate is sin – is to be complete in this state of probation. This is the hope it sees set before us in the Gospel, and this, therefore, it presses upon the pursuit and attainment of all who are in Christ. This is, in the judgment of many, its specific heresy; this, in its own judgment, is its specific glory . . .

Source: William Burt Pope, 'Methodist Doctrine', *The Wesley Memorial Volume* ed J. O. A. Clark, New York 1880, p. 189.

With justice, it may be claimed that, up until his time, Pope presented the best formulation of Methodist Arminianism in coherent, amicable and well-structured form. He brought nineteenth-century Methodist theology to finely accomplished statement. The past he presented well, but the future would have to be different; Methodism could not continue to live so isolated from its intellectual, social and cultural contexts.

For discussion

1. John Wesley attempted to secure Methodist doctrine by referring to his *Notes on the New Testament* and his four volumes of sermons. To what extent is it possible to fix doctrines in this way and prevent it from changing?

2. What are your own 'core convictions'? How do they compare with Adam Clarke's?

3. Langford contrasts Richard Watson's view of the authority of scripture with that of John Wesley. How do you understand the authority of the Bible?

4. For William Arthur, preaching the Christian gospel was inseparable from arguing the Christian case. How far is the relationship between these two activities properly appreciated today? Ought the Decade of Evangelism to be twinned with a Decade of Apologetics?

5. Langford suggests that nineteenth-century Methodism was 'an enclosed tradition'. How far is this true of Methodism today?

3
Methodist Theology in North America

Its early character

The spread of Methodism was linked with the growth of the British Empire. It is an English-language tradition, as Lutheranism is a German-language tradition. So now we move beyond Great Britain in order to offer a glimpse of the international range of Methodism and the variety of its theological formations. In North America, Methodism grew to prominence as its work of evangelism and the development of Christian character was extended, first across the ocean and then across the continent. Direct indebtedness to John Wesley and nourishment from British Methodism were important elements in this development; nevertheless, as we shall see, Methodism in different cultural settings took on distinctive characteristics.

In the 1760s Methodism was carried to America, primarily by lay people from Ireland. But what amounted to a fresh start was made after the war which won, for the American colonies, independence from the British Crown. In 1780 the membership was not large enough to show on the national census, but forty-five years later, in 1825, Methodism was the largest Protestant body in the United States. This remarkable growth was due to many factors but perhaps chiefly to the evangelical zeal of the Methodists, the potency of their message and the cultural and personal readiness of the populace to receive it.

What, then, was the message? The central themes were repentance and faith, justification and forgiveness, and Christian perfection. Emphasis was on the change of life which is expressed in the inner experience of transformation and the external witness of moral living. The mission which the movement attempted – 'to spread scriptural holiness over the land' – was fulfilled in evangelism, and the response was immense. The Methodist movement began to make its distinctive imprint on the nation, and continued to do so for more than a century.

Theologically the themes were simple. Individuals were asked a couple of fundamental questions about their spiritual experience: Do you accept Jesus Christ as your Lord and Saviour? Do you accept the Old and New Testaments as the guides to life? There was also the expectation that life begun in justification would mature over time, or in a moment, into a perfect love of God.[1]

Expanded theological interpretations were a consequence, not a foundation, of this experience. John Wesley had abridged the articles of faith of the Church of England and had provided the Methodist Episcopal Church in North America with essential Articles of Religion. These articles provided a framework to guide and support faith; belief in these articles was not the condition of faith, yet these interpretations were provided in order to enrich faith already experienced.

Theological education for early nineteenth-century North American Methodist ministers was a Course of Study which required individual preparation and the passing of tests administered by ordained Preachers. There was no emphasis on formally educated ministers. Indeed, early Methodist educational institutions were for laity; they were not – as in the Reformed tradition – originally established to educate clergy. Theological authors were, therefore, self-educated and wrote about the gospel to be preached and lived. A practical theological emphasis, with little interest in formal theological treatises or systematic theological statements, continued.

In spite of challenges, especially the difficulty of doing theology as only part of a more inclusive life of ministry, there were some who attempted to reflect on the interpretation of faith. The modes of their writing were most often articles and pamphlets, and they used theology to undergird the initiation and practice of Christian faith.

Chief among the voices of North American Methodism were Nathan Bangs and Francis Asbury.

Francis Asbury

Francis Asbury (1745–1816), an Englishman sent by John Wesley, became the primary shaper of Methodism on the North American continent. He was the first bishop, and remained important until his death. Asbury was the preacher and organizer of the expanding movement and it is almost impossible to overstate his influence; he energized, guided, motivated, and embodied the order of the new church. In his person he exemplified the essential qualities of the movement. Theologically, he continued Wesleyan themes by preaching for conversion and Christian holiness, and his passion ignited a fire that burned across the land.

Nathan Bangs

Nathan Bangs (1778–1862) was the most influential theological spokesman.[2] Born in Connecticut, he moved to Western New York state, then Canada,

then back to New York. In 1820, he became the Book Editor of the Methodist Book Concern. He had been writing since 1809, in spite of little formal education, and he participated directly in the philosophical and theological discussions of the era. It is significant that Bangs edited the complete works of Thomas Reid, the leader of the Scottish Common Sense school of philosophy, which was dominant at Princeton, Harvard, and Yale and which stressed the continuity between the human mind and the real world, the unity of truth, the rationality of the world, and the reality of God providing order to the whole. The significance of Bangs' editing of these works is that it demonstrates his engagement in the contemporary intellectual culture. For Bangs' interest was in the intellectual context in which the gospel must be preached and, through Bangs, Methodism in North America became a participant in the intellectual issues of the day.

Bangs, a contemporary of Adam Clarke and Richard Watson in England, was also the editor of *The Methodist Magazine* (from 1820), established *The Christian Advocate* (1826) and served as editor for the *Methodist Magazine and Quarterly Review* (1832–36). In these publications as well as in several books, he attempted to preserve and present the Wesleyan dynamic of free grace and free will. He did this most extensively in *Errors of Hopkinsianism* (1815) and *Predestination Examined* (1817). The fight was with a Calvinism which so stressed God's sovereignty that, Bangs believed, the moral integrity of both God and human beings was lost. He intended to keep grace primary and so he stressed prevenient grace, rooted in the atonement of Jesus Christ and present to all people. Only prevenient grace makes human response possible and, because there is prevenient grace, freedom, which had been lost at the Fall, is given back and can be used in either acceptance or rejection of the gospel.

Both Calvinism and Methodism were revival movements in North America; indeed, Perry Miller has claimed that the chief character of American culture was the revivalism which dominated the first six decades of the nineteenth century. The revivalists, though apparently involved in a common – and remarkably successful – endeavour, were often, in practice, in mutually destructive competition. In such a situation, all participants were forced to clarify their positions and give theological accounts of their convictions.

Nathan Bangs stated the Methodist position: human beings are thoroughly sinful and unable to save themselves, but the prevenient grace of God comes with seeking and enabling power [30]. Bangs moved the discussion from the eternal decrees of God to the historical consequences of the cross and from deterministic control of human action to utilization of the new freedom granted by God. Grace is present because of Jesus Christ's historical atonement, and response to that atoning work provides forgiveness of sin and new power in the Holy Spirit to live a Christian life.

---

30. In an age of scientific advance, predicated upon scientific models of tight cause-and-effect relationships, the effort to find an alternative model [for the relationship between God and human beings] was exceedingly difficult; but it was this issue that Methodist theologians pursued throughout the better part of the century. In this endeavour the doctrine of prevenient grace assumed basic significance.

Source: Thomas A. Langford, *Practical Divinity*, Abingdon 1983, p. 85.

Changing emphases

Methodist theology in North America in the nineteenth century went through three major phases: establishing itself within the intellectual/theological discussions of its day; asserting its distinctive emphasis upon Christian holiness; and developing extensive systematic theological statements in multiple volumes. No neat historical divisions may be drawn, but the first era roughly covered the first third of the century. Nathan Bangs, as we have indicated, was the chief representative of the initial period; Phoebe Palmer and Bangs represented the emphasis of the middle years;

and Thomas O. Summers and John Miley were the chief figures in the closing decades.

One of the most distinctive characteristics of Methodism was its emphasis on Christian holiness or the perfect love of God. Both Wesleys had placed great stress on this theme and it was continued by the movement in general. In North America, emphasis on revival was so insistent that there seemed to be some diminution of preaching about sanctification. But the concern for spiritual maturation continued even as its proponents struggled to provide adequate interpretation of the experience.

Phoebe Palmer

A renewal of holiness interest was given impetus in the mid-1830s through the influence of Phoebe Palmer (1807–1874). Arising from a series of 'Tuesday meetings' in the mid-1830s in New York, organized by her sister, Sarah A. Lankford, Phoebe Palmer raised the question: Is there not a 'shorter way' to the realization of Christian perfection? The accepted, 'longer' way involved waiting upon the witness of the Holy Spirit which conveyed inner assurance that God was loved with a whole heart. This way, however, was uncontrollable, could lead to uncertainty about the relationship, and could seem to wax and wane over time. The issue was: How can anyone know for sure that they are in this special relationship with God?

As an alternative, Palmer proposed that a more certain, less tenuous, knowledge could come from scriptural promises, namely, that God has said that complete dedication would issue in holiness. Hence, we need to accept what God has promised; that is, we should place everything upon the altar ('altar' language was very important in the movement) and, through this dedication, sanctification would be accomplished [31]. Palmer wrote of her experience (she wrote in the third person): 'Instead of perceiving anything meritorious in what she had been enabled, through grace, to do, i.e. in laying all upon the altar, she saw that she had but rendered back to God that which was already his own . . . *Faith is taking God at His word, relying unwaveringly upon His truth.*'³

31. It was thus, that by 'laying all upon this altar', she by the most unequivocal Scripture testimony, as she deemed, laid herself under the most sacred obligation to believe that the sacrifice became 'holy and acceptable', and virtually the *Lord's property*, even by virtue of the sanctity of the altar upon which it was laid, and continued 'holy and acceptable', so long as kept inviolably upon this hallowed altar.

Source: Phoebe Palmer, *The Way of Holiness*, New York 1850, p. 65.

32. By Methodist I understood those peculiarities of the system by which it is distinguished from all other *isms*; hence it not only included the doctrines [characteristic of general Protestant theology] enumerated above, by which it proves its orthodoxy, but it brings out more prominently than is done in other denominations . . . that of Christian perfection, or the entire sanctification of the whole of man to God, or holiness of heart and life.

Source: Nathan Bangs, *The Present State and Prospects and Responsibilities of The Methodist Episcopal Church*, New York 1850, pp. 58–59.

The concern was to replace what Palmer took to be a subjective assurance with a more objective base. For her the sequence was clear: if persons would place full confidence in God's promises, God would fulfill those promises. It is important to note that Palmer's method of beginning with scripture and using the biblical word to shape experience was in direct keeping with Richard Watson's move which made scripturally-based propositions the foundation of Christian experience. Rather than scripture interpreting experience, scripture frames experience and determines the form it should take.

The impact of Phoebe Palmer's approach was immediate and wide-ranging; there was a renewal of interest in the doctrine of Christian holiness. This holiness teaching issued in conferences and camp meetings where purity of love and purity of heart were central themes. This was also contemporary with the impact of William Arthur's influential writing in Great Britain, an impact which spread also to North America. A new holiness movement was underway, one which would later depart from episcopal Methodism and establish a series of denominations on the North American continent.

But there were, for some, serious theological questions about Palmer's method. Among those who raised questions was Nathan Bangs [32]. Bangs welcomed the newly-energized interest in this distinctive Methodist doctrine. But he believed that the move from the direct experience of the Holy Spirit changed the essential understanding of the Wesleyan doctrine.

Palmer's method, he argued, made the process too mechanical, too predictable and, in all, too simple.

In episcopal Methodism Bangs' interpretation became standard and was endorsed by major leaders such as Randolf S. Foster, Professor of Theology at Boston University and later a bishop. The witness of the spirit remained fundamental; a basic emphasis on a specific 'second work of grace' was questioned [33].

33. It is well, nay, it is indispensable, to make an entire surrender of all to God; and when this is done, God will acknowledge it by sending the witness of his acceptance, but let no one, at his peril, conclude that he has made this surrender, and is consequently sanctified, without the requisite witness; he will only deceive himself, and receive no benefit. His faith, however strong, being false, will do him no good. It is the Spirit which sanctifies, and he sanctifies through faith – faith not in any act of ours, but faith in God; and when by faith he sanctifies, he will impart the witness.

Source: Randolf S. Foster, *Christian Purity*, New York 1869, p. 206.

Splits were occurring as new holiness movements were spawned, and then issued in divisions within the church. Not only did earlier emerging denominations, such as Wesleyan Methodists and Free Methodists, make sanctification central, but The Church of the Nazarene and Pentecostal groups also established separate identities. By the end of the century North American Methodism was fragmented over interpretation of this doctrine.

The centrally contested issue was the mode of the Holy Spirit's operation. In episcopal Methodism, the emphasis was upon the immediate working of the Spirit, while according to Phoebe Palmer the Holy Spirit was conveyed by the scriptural word. For her, the Holy Spirit was mediated, while according to her opponents the Spirit was directly present to each individual. Again, the relation of scripture and Christian experience was at stake.

It is historically significant that in mid-century there was the crisis over slavery and racism. By the 1840s the nation was pulling apart, and the Methodist Episcopal Church split between the North (The Methodist Episcopal Church) and the South (The Methodist Episcopal Church, South). Different attitudes towards slavery were not rooted in clear differences of theological interest or interpretation. Both Methodist churches, in fact, consistently agreed in their opposition to slavery and the *Discipline* of the Methodist Episcopal Church, South, continued to prohibit slave holding among Methodists. The difference was in the attitude to or understanding of the relation of church moral standards to civil law. In the South, as the *Discipline* stated, the civil law took priority over church standards. Although, therefore, the northern church was more affected by the holiness movement and the southern church was more conservative in polity, theologically there was fundamental agreement.[4]

Systematic theology

Wesleyan Methodism in the United States took on a more formal character in the last quarter of the nineteenth century. Until that time, theology was clearly subservient to the practical task of preaching for conversion and growth in holiness. Theological spokespersons were editors, preachers serving congregations and a few presidents or professors in colleges. Until 1860 there were no graduate theological courses and no people who held academic positions whose primary task was to think, teach and write about theology.

In the last three decades of the nineteenth century, more formal modes of theological education issued in the writing of sustained theological texts. Two people exemplified this move, Thomas O. Summers (1812–1882) at Vanderbilt who represented the Methodist Episcopal Church, South and John Miley (1813–1895) at Boston University who represented the Methodist Episcopal Church. Both of these men, from different perspectives, produced systematic theologies and attempted to give Methodist theology formal and comprehensive expression. Summers undertook this task by cautiously updating Richard Watson's *Theological Institutes*.

Thomas O. Summers

Thomas Summers was an immigrant from England who became the Editor of the Methodist Episcopal Church, South's publication concern. He wrote on many topics and eventually became the first professor of theology at the newly established Vanderbilt University. He was basically influenced by the Scottish Common Sense philosophy which was then dominant on the American scene. Natural reason and revelation provided a unity of knowledge and upon this foundation was built a comprehensive interpretation of God, the world, and human beings. The position provided a confident assurance about the rationality of the world and of the Christian message. The theologian's task was to offer a clear, systematic statement which comprehends the existence of God, the meaning of the world and the place of human beings in the created order. God and reality were a homogenous whole. Friction was caused by failure to articulate these interconnections rather than by any fundamental conflict or inherent contradiction. The name given this position was 'rational orthodoxy', and both words carried full weight.

Thomas Summers inherited these convictions and confidently built upon them. In 1888 he produced a two volume *Systematic Theology* which was an extended presentation of Richard Watson's arguments and conclusions. Of more concern than atheism were the Deists, who acknowledged God's existence but did not accept the special doctrines of Christian faith, especially the unique revelation of God in Jesus Christ. It was to the inclusion of these themes that Summers paid special attention. He was thorough but not original. Deeply fearful of heresy, he took Watson as the standard of 'right doctrine'.

Summers' style was abrupt, his convictions conservative and his demeanour, on occasion, abrasive and overbearing, but he represented a strongly-expressed assurance about the rationality and convincing power of Christian faith. Summers did not so much advance understanding of Christian faith as consolidate received interpretation; he gave expression to what was believed and, as such, spoke more for his time than to his time.

It is not certain how dependent Methodist preachers were upon the formal articulation of faith and how much they were influenced by evangelism and its continuing, but changing, concern with Christian holiness. In so far as Summers gave voice to what was common conviction, the power of received teaching seems to dominate Methodist preaching and thinking. Certainly in the Methodist Episcopal Church, South there was a strong spirit of traditionalism and a desire to perpetuate their inheritance in preaching and shaping life. This conservative impulse would continue into the early twentieth century.

Robert E. Chiles, in a revealing study,[5] has argued that North American Methodism underwent a deterioration through its first one hundred and fifty years, from Watson to John Miley to Albert Knudson. The themes he develops are: from revelation to reason; from sinful man to moral man; from free grace to free will. In each of these cases, Chiles sees a significant change from Wesley's primary dependence upon God to an optimistic view of human potentiality and possibility. Wesley was being reinterpreted until the tradition was made fully compatible with the dominant Protestant liberalism.

John Miley

The work of John Miley (1813–1895) is significant in two ways. On the one hand, he forged the contributions of his Methodist predecessors into a new synthesis; on the other hand, his work represented a concluding statement of that tradition and thereby made evident a need for new directions. To put the matter another way, he was fair and favourable to his predecessors and brought their work to a fine but final expression. Beyond him, however, and among his own colleagues at Boston University, new philosophical and theological approaches were being used to engage a changing culture. After Miley, Methodism was opened to new voices and willingly listened to them.

Nevertheless, his achievement must not be minimized. Because he was clear, careful and constructive, a century's theological endeavour came to a strong conclusion. Miley named his system 'ethical Arminianism', and by this he meant to stress, in keeping with traditional Methodist emphases, God's free grace and human free will. God acts 'ethically' by respecting the integrity of human life: God is not an autocrat who exercises irresistible power; rather he deals interactively with human beings. At the same time, persons in relation to God also have responsibility to act ethically in relation to other persons. Ethical Arminianism was a systematic effort to express the meaning of the two great commandments.

Philosophically and sympathetically, Miley was committed to universal awareness of God. Direct experience of God is possible for all persons and constitutes the foundation upon which theological interpretation is built. But Christian scripture is inerrant and primary as the norm of interpretation, and therefore what is known primarily but inchoately through nature may be known most truly through scriptural witness.

Philosophically, Miley was convinced that truth is a whole so that science and religion, revelation and reason, are compatible and each needs the other for full rational articulation. One of his major efforts was to show the complementary interplay between these two dimensions of reality. He argued vigorously against those who, from either side, excluded the other, and so opposed both positivistic views of science and isolated religious affirmation. Completeness of vision and understanding was possible only as one combined the distinctive contributions from both sides.

In regard to scriptural interpretation, Miley held to the authority of an infallible God-given scriptural word. He was careful not to credit inspiration that came from human genius. His own position he called a 'dynamical theory', that is, he stressed the interaction of God and human beings under the guidance of the Holy Spirit. In contrast to Calvinist emphasis upon the biblical words *per se*, Miley stressed that scripture, perfect as it is, can only be the word of God and carry the authority of God by the work of the Holy Spirit. In this he represented the dominant view of Methodist theologians in the late nineteenth century.

In his efforts to bring inherited Methodist theology to a culmination, Miley tended towards a primary emphasis on free personal agency and in this he continued to over-balance the free-grace, free-will tension towards human responsibility. Nevertheless, through the entire two-volume *Systematic Theology* he deals with all the major Christian and Wesleyan themes and presents Christian doctrine as a coherent whole.

Miley brought the tradition he had received to comprehensive statement. His work showed singular thoroughness in presenting Methodist theology, but it also marked the end of an era. By the turn of the century new philosophical persuasions were prominent, new cultural assumptions were shaping North America, new understandings were proposed as more appropriate for Christian witness. The leadership of this new movement came from Miley's own setting, Boston University, and 'Boston Personalism' became synonymous with American Methodist theology.

Within the North American cultural context new issues drew attention away from an insular theological community. One of the most distinct and thorough influences in Western culture from the middle of the nineteenth century until the present has been the emphasis on history, on the historicity of human existence and the history of texts and artifacts of human thought and life. Hence the developing character of human life, the historical nature of scripture and the historical role of God were forced to centre stage. Underwriting and reinforcing this awareness were the scientific interpretations of the cosmos at both its macroscopic and microscopic levels. Christian theology faced a changing world and had to meet it with new philosophical and historical tools.

Transition

The change in Methodist theology at the end of the century was pronounced. Albert Knudson stated the differences with great clarity as he discussed the move from John Miley to Henry Clay Sheldon. Sheldon was a colleague of Miley and then succeeded him as systematic theologian at Boston University, but the differences between them were marked.[6]

Henry Clay Sheldon

Henry Clay Sheldon (1845–1928), who published *The Essentials of Christianity* in 1922, inaugurated a change [34] which was brought to full fruition by his more significant successors, Borden Parker Bowne and Albert C. Knudson. Sheldon's contribution, according to Knudson, arose from two basic judgments: first, that the earlier Methodist theologians, from Watson to Pope to Miley, did not recognize the importance of vital experience in Methodism and therefore

---

34. The newer theology, represented by Sheldon, is also more rational than the older in that it tends to limit revelation to the religious realm and denies to it a coercive power over the human reason. It allows to science its full rights and does not attempt in the name of religion to impose upon the modern man the imperfect scientific notions found in the Bible.

Source: A. C. Knudson, 'Henry Clay Sheldon – Theologian', *The Methodist Review*, March 1925, Vol. XLI, p. 180.

could not do justice to its true genius; and, second, that they had not adjusted themselves to the new developments in biblical criticism.

The previous theologians therefore were, in Knudson's terminology, 'authoritarian rationalists'. As they formulated the central doctrines of the Christian faith, experience was, for them, always secondary to scripture. Sheldon, on the other hand, does not treat revelation as 'an objective verity unrelated to experience. It is conditioned both in its nature and range by faith.'[7]

A second major difference between Sheldon and his predecessors relates to the doctrines of the Trinity and christology. The change was evident in the focus upon human personality and away from theoretical abstractions. In Sheldon, 'we manifestly have a step in the direction of anthropocentric as distinguished from a theocentric christology, but only a step . . . he may be regarded as leaving the door open to those who feel constrained to move further in the anthropocentric direction than he himself does . . .'[8]

Finally, both in his treatment of the atonement and in his idea of divine immanence, Sheldon moves beyond his Methodist predecessors. In regard to the atonement, he moved away from both the satisfaction and the governmental theories and towards a moral influence theory, stressing more fully the subjective, receptive side of the new relation between God and human beings as effected by Jesus Christ. Where immanence is concerned, as Knudson notes, 'It was Sheldon who first introduced into Methodist systematic theology the idealistic viewpoint with its conception of the divine immanence.'[9]

A fundamental change had occurred. North American Methodist theology was loosened from its previous moorings and was now set upon a new adventure, engaging a new philosophical, scientific world.

Borden Parker Bowne

Within Methodism, the major figure in this transition was Borden Parker Bowne (1847–1910).[10] Bowne was the intellectual leader of North American Meth-

odism and founded at Boston University a wide-ranging philosophical theology which he called 'Personalism'. Upon this base he established a 'school' of theology, the only broad ranging mode of interpretation ever established within Methodism. The perspective of 'Boston Personalism' was adopted by philosophers, such as Edgar Brightman, and theologians, such as Albert C. Knudson and L. Harold DeWolf, as well as by biblical scholars, personality theorists and church administrators. This school dominated North American Methodist theology for the first half of the twentieth century.

For Bowne, this form of idealistic philosophy changed the emphasis from transcendence to immanence and from a cosmic impersonal void to personality as the central character of reality [35].

---

35. The undivineness of the natural and the unnaturalness of the divine is the great heresy of popular thought . . . To assist in the banishment of this error by showing a more excellent way is the aim and purpose of this little book.

Source: Borden Parker Bowne, *The Immanence of God*, New York 1905, preface.

The theological base was essential: God is the most real Being and God is personal. Hence personality is the ultimate category [36]. Upon this foundation Bowne reinterprets the nature of God, the role of Jesus Christ, human nature, the character and message of scripture and the final hope and destiny of the world. From the assertion of God as person, to the

---

36. A succinct definition of Personalism:

That form of idealism which gives actual recognition to both the pluralistic and monistic aspects of experience and which finds in the conscious unity, identity and free activity of personality the key to the nature of reality and the solution of the ultimate problems of philosophy.

Source: Albert C. Knudson, *The Philosophy of Personalism*, Boston 1927, p. 87.

---

significance of human persons in relation to God and one another, to the role of Jesus Christ as exemplar and culminator of that relationship, to scripture as an expression of these presuppositions and to belief in historical progress which will find its fruition in divine/human community, the position was comprehensive and dynamic. Fresh creative interpretation was made in all of these areas.

Emphasis on the immanence of God establishes a closeness of God and human beings. As a consequence, the idea of a radical break caused by sin is countered by an interpretation which stresses continuity between the Divine and human. Related to this is a re-evaluation of the role of Jesus Christ who does not so much bring new creation as a true understanding of the actual and existing character of reality. Scripture, which is historically shaped, gives expression to personal relations and provides the fundamental statement of the meaning of the experience of humankind with Divine presence. Reality is continuous, and upon this base Bowne develops a natural theology.

Bowne provides a Methodist presentation of the assumptions of the Christian liberalism which was culturally dominant in the West at the beginning of the twentieth century. Liberalism, which was a positive force in shaping the Christian mission for its era, stressed the homogenous relation of science and religion, of reason and revelation and of human and divine destiny.

From his Methodist heritage Bowne derives his idea of God as grace and embeds grace into the nature of reality, that is, in God as person and in God as immanent in all created relationships. Theology is rooted in theism into which are placed understandings of Jesus Christ, human nature and historical hope. To support this position, Bowne felt it especially important to counter both materialistic and mechanistic interpretations of reality (as represented, for example, by Herbert Spencer, upon whose thought he taught a seminar almost every year) and those forms of idealism which moved toward impersonal understandings of reality.

In spite of his serious philosophical effort, Bowne did not look to philosophy or ordinary rational experience to produce specifically Christian experience. Rather he emphasizes, from his own revivalistic background, the instigation of awareness and appropriation of Divine-human relationships as exemplified and communicated through Jesus Christ. Hence, through the enlightenment of a special experience, one is opened to the reality of God and to an initiation of comprehensive understanding.

Bowne was also important in changing the prevailing Methodist attitude towards the authority of scripture. In this Bowne supported and was supported by a general intellectual ethos. Historical awareness was, once again, the foundation of new interpretation. German higher critical study of scripture was making inroads into North American biblical study, and by the last decades of the nineteenth century this was reflected in Methodism. Bowne made a distinctive contribution by providing a philosophical foundation and theological interpretation which underwrote the possibility and the significance of such a mode of interpretation. He provided a context in which the presence and relationship of the Holy Spirit was central to biblical understanding.

The impact of Bowne was enormous. Personalistic philosophical theology became a dominant character of Methodist theology and this interpretation carried the church into the twentieth century with a passionate concern for human life and for relating in creative and contributory ways to its culture.

Response and challenge

The influence of Boston Personalism continued with vigour after the mid-twentieth century. The significance of the Boston Personalists in shaping Methodist intellectual sensibilities was thoroughly permeative; nevertheless there were eventually challengers from within Methodism who fundamentally questioned the presuppositions of personalism.

Edwin Lewis

Chief among these challengers was Edwin Lewis (1881–1959) of Drew University, who for more than a decade – in the 1920s – thought and wrote as a personalistic theologian. In the early 1930s, however, under the influence of 'Christian realists' such as Reinhold Niebuhr and continental thinkers such as Karl Barth, Lewis became convinced of the radical sinfulness of human beings and of the basic recreation of human life by Jesus Christ effected by the atonement. In *A Christian Manifesto* (1934)[11] he expressed his dismay at the assumptions of liberal Christianity (which he had shared through the decade of the 1920s) and began positively to contruct a view of Jesus Christ as redeemer and creator of new human life [37].

---

37. Let us be done with compromise, and let us affirm – affirm magnificently, affirm audaciously. Let us affirm God – his unchanging love for men, his unchanging hatred of sin, his sacrificial presence in all the life and work of Jesus. Let us affirm Christ – Christ as the meaning of God. Christ as what God is in virtue of the mysterious 'kenosis' by which he made himself one with a human life, and at the same time that he was doing the utmost he could do for men endured the worst – a Cross – that men could do against him. Let us affirm the Spirit – the divine concern to bring to bear upon the hearts and consciences of men the impact of what God in Christ has done and is forever doing on their behalf, to the end that they may be moved to repentance, to that faith which ensures forgiveness, to that love which brings moral empowerment, and to that surrender of the will which makes God's purposes their purpose.

Source: Edwin Lewis, 'The Fatal Apostasy of the Modern Church', *Religion In Life*, Autumn 1933, p. 491.

The idea of evil dominated Lewis' thought and led him eventually to affirm a dualism between good and evil, God and satanic powers.[12] His own seriousness about the reality of evil, both as sin and as cosmic force, led him to a special and rather isolated position. But he was important as a transitional figure in North American Methodism and created space for the resuscitation of more classical Protestant themes.

Revival of interest in John Wesley

A separate but corroborating development – a revival of interest in Wesley himself – added to the criticism of the liberal tradition which Boston Personalism represented. An effort was made to move behind recent interpretations of John Wesley, such as Umphrey Lee's, *John Wesley and Modern Religion*, to a study of Wesleyan texts themselves and an attempt to exegete these primary sources.

The leading figures of this new investigation were the Scandinavian theologian, Harald Lindstrom, author of *John Wesley and Sanctification* (1943), William R. Cannon, author of *The Theology of John Wesley* (1946), and the editors associated with the Wesley Works project, such as Frank Baker, Albert C. Outler and Robert E. Cushman. This renewal of interest in John Wesley indicated a general re-appropriation of classical Protestant theological themes such as the Trinity, human sinfulness, Jesus Christ as the mediator of new creation, Christian discipleship and the priority of grace in the tension between free grace and free will.

This group initiated an effort to produce a complete edition of the works of John Wesley. The scheme began in 1959 and is continuing until today. The entire set will comprise some thirty-five volumes and contain the most important writings of Wesley, including his sermons, letters, journals, hymns and occasional writings. This project continues to feed an important stream of Methodist theology.

The principal aim of this project is to establish the best possible text of Wesley's writings. Exhaustive attention has been paid to finding and comparing all available texts. This textual work has been so thorough that it should never need to be done again. Introductions and commentaries are also provided and represent the best current Wesley scholarship. This interpretative work will be ongoing and require continual reassessment. The present achievement is monumental and provides an essential resource for continuing study of John Wesley.

Process Theology

Shortly after mid-century another distinctive movement came to explicit and strong expression in the United States, especially among Methodist theologians. This was denominated 'Process Thought' or 'Process Theology'. The background figures were Alfred North Whitehead and Charles Hartshorne. Methodist theological leadership has been provided by John B. Cobb, Jr. (1925–) and Schubert M. Ogden (1928–).

These two men, faithful to this philosophical persuasion but also of clear intellectual independence, have probed especially the doctrine of God. Moreover, seeing God as continuous creativity, they have explored the implications of this view for understanding human nature, christology, the Holy Spirit, and prayer and its ethical consequences for ecology, liberation, social reconstruction and personal growth. Ogden's definitions of some key theological terms are given below [38].

---

38. *Redemption*, 'the unique process of God's self actualization, whereby he creatively synthesizes all other things into his own actual being as God'.

Sin, 'the rejection of ourselves and the creatures we know ourselves to be.'

Salvation, 'the process that includes not only the redeeming action of God himself but also the faithful response to this action on the part of the individual sinner.'

Emancipation, 'the fullest possible self-realization [of every creature].'

Source: Schubert M. Ogden, *Faith And Freedom*, Nashville 1979, pp. 83, 86, 87, 90.

Process Thought has been a continuation of liberal Protestant thought within Methodism and has provided an engagement with a contemporary intellectual enterprise. Once again, the complexity and diversity of North American Methodist theology is made clear.

As Methodism entered the last quarter of the century, its theology displayed several different thrusts which, despite their uncertain future, continued with some strength. The influence of Personalism, now mixed with other philosophical trends, persisted. Recovery of John

Wesley's thought continued, thanks to a sensed need for Methodist self-identity. And Process Thought reached its climax in the work of John B. Cobb, Jr and Schubert M. Ogden. Diversity, in short, characterizes theology in the United Methodist Church.

The final decades of the twentieth century present some changes whose contributions are yet to be known. Several parallel trends seem prominent: the reconnecting of theology with ethics, the setting of theology within the context of world religions and different cultural/language settings, establishment of chairs of evangelism in theological schools, and biblical interpretation set within the context of new styles of critical literary study. Moreover, a number of developments illustrate sensitivity to the diversity of the church's life: the publication of a Spanish language ritual (1984), a new hymn book for United Methodism (1989) and a new Book of Worship (1992) as well as a hymn book in the Korean language (1994). At present, in fact, American Methodism lives with a sense of its inclusiveness of life and thought.

A revision of the Book of Discipline

In 1988 the General Conference of the United Methodist Church adopted a theological statement which was a complete rewriting of its official position. This rewriting represented a major new section (Part II) of the *Discipline* and was adopted with an overwhelming and enthusiastic endorsement. This statement represents where now the United Methodist Church understands itself to be.

Under the general title of 'Doctrinal Standards and Our Theological Task', the statement is divided into five major parts: 'Our Doctrinal Heritage', 'Our Doctrinal History', 'Our Doctrinal Standards and General Rules', 'Our Theological Task', and 'Mission Statement'. Each section is important.

The statement begins with an affirmation of the common heritage which all Christians have in the mystery of salvation in Jesus Christ, transmitted by the Holy Spirit and experienced among the community of believers; the statement affirms the Church universal, the reign of God, and the authority of scripture.

39. Our heritage in doctrine and our present theological task focus upon a renewed grasp of the sovereignty of God and of God's love in Christ amid the continuing crises of human existence.

Our forebears in the faith reaffirmed the ancient Christian message as found in the apostolic witness, even as they applied it anew to their own circumstances.

Their preaching and teaching were grounded in Scripture, informed by Christian tradition, enlivened in experience, and tested by reason.

Their labours inspire and inform our attempts to convey the saving gospel to our world with its needs and aspirations.

Source: *The Book of Discipline of the United Methodist Church*, 1992, p. 40.

Next there is a restatement of distinctive Methodist emphases: prevenient grace, justification and assurance, sanctification and perfection, faith and good works, mission and service. These two dimensions – of the universal church with its larger, more inclusive truth and the Methodist tradition with its special emphases – are deliberately bound together. Indeed, this joining of the larger Christian tradition with its own tradition is typical of United Methodist understanding [39]. The section concludes by combining the interaction of doctrine and discipline in Christian life [40].

40. Wesley's orientation toward the practical is evident in his focus upon the 'scripture way of salvation'. He considered doctrinal matters primarily in terms of their significance for Christian discipleship.

The Wesleyan emphasis upon the Church life – faith and love put into practice – has been the hallmark of those traditions now incorporated into The United Methodist Church. The distinctive shape of the Wesleyan theological heritage can be seen in a constellation of doctrinal emphases that display the creating, redeeming, and sanctifying activity of God.

Source: *The Book of Discipline of the United Methodist Church*, 1992, p. 44.

'Our Doctrinal History' is a recounting of the doctrinal 'standards' in Great Britain, in North America and among the various Methodist traditions in both of these geographical areas. The effort is to set these doctrinal statements in their context and to preserve them as important parts of the ongoing Methodist tradition.

'Our Theological Task' is particularly important [41] as the statement undertakes to indicate the setting of contemporary theological effort. The context is complex and must be seen whole: namely, as individual and communal, as contextual and incarnational, and as essentially practical. Even more important is the discussion of the quadrilateral which is used to develop Christian understanding: namely, scripture, tradition, reason and experience. Each of these sources is discussed in order to set their priority and interaction.

41. In the name of Jesus Christ we are called to work within our diversity while exercising patience and forbearance with one another. Such patience stems neither from indifference towards truth nor from an indulgent tolerance of error but from an awareness that we know only in part and that none of us is able to search the mysteries of God except by the Spirit of God. We proceed with our theological task trusting that the Spirit will grant us wisdom to continue our journey with the whole people of God.

Source: *The Book of Discipline of the United Methodist Church*, 1992, p. 83.

This section concludes with a reaffirmation of Methodism's ecumenical openness and commitment to Christian unity. In this spirit, the theological task is described: 'We endeavor through the power of the Holy Spirit to understand the love of God given in Jesus Christ. We seek to spread this love abroad.'[13]

The theological task concludes with a mission statement. This is appropriate in view of the fundamental nature of Methodist understanding of the church and of its special calling to spread scriptural holiness. The challenge is to bear witness to God's grace by proclamation, evangelization, calling all persons into the body of Christ and service as God's servants to all people and the whole of creation.

This statement is important as it draws together the corporate agreement of the United Methodist Church at this time. The effort to keep the rich inheritance from the past along with the intense desire to forge new understanding and service in the present combines reception and openness. Much has been given, much remains to be done.

This document also represents a corporate statement by the church. In discussing theology a distinction is made in the document between exploratory theology and doctrinal theology. The difference is that exploratory theology represents the reach of the church as led by individual theologians who seek new possibilities. Doctrine is the grasp of the church as represented by corporate judgment about possibilities for inclusion into its body of faith. A living church must have free and rich exploration; a vibrant church must choose among possibilities and build its doctrinal house upon bases of common agreement. The total theological statement presents the corporate wisdom and doctrinal conviction of the United Methodist Church.

This quick survey is provided to give a sense of the range of development of Methodist theology. Though the tradition has moved across continents and has taken on a variety of embodiments, some recognizable characteristics have persisted. There is no need to attempt to display family resemblances or unlikeness. But in different cultural settings, even within a single national culture, Methodism has persistently attempted to understand and express its mission as given by the initial impulse from John Wesley.

Interactions between British Methodism and North American Methodism have been cordial and there is a positive relationship. But distinctive character development is obvious and theological conversation takes place with an awareness of both common interest and different responsibilities.[14]

For discussion

1. In what ways has North American Methodist theology differed from that of British Methodism? What can we learn from this theology?
2. One distinctive feature of North American Methodism was its emphasis on holiness. What has this to offer us – or warn us against – today?
3. The chapter contrasts 'the assumptions of Christian liberalism' and 'the classical Protestant themes'. Try to spell out the meaning of both phrases, perhaps using other resources. Can any theologian with a revivalist background be typically Liberal or typically Protestant?
4. In the chapter, the revival of interest in John Wesley is associated with criticism of the liberal tradition. How does this relate to the 'elusive Mr Wesley', portrayed in chapter 1?
5. In the light of the 1988 theological statement of the United Methodist Church, compile your own version of 'Doctrinal Standards and Our Theological Task'.

4

Times of Change

British Methodism shared in the general religious culture at the end of the nineteenth century. It was therefore affected by several intertwined issues which produced a dramatic change in the national setting. The central issue was that of authority: what are the foundations of religious convictions, in terms of both thought and action? By the last decade of the century there was a general rejection of dogmatic theology[1] and a renewal of effort to relate Christian faith to contemporary cultural and societal conditions. John W. Grant states that there was impatience with concentration on inherited dogma and the continuing restatement of received doctrine. 'The challenge to faith presented by science and criticism [of the scripture], the new interest in the history of religion, and the demand for the reform of the life of England left little room for the pure theologian.'[2] During the last decade of the nineteenth century and the first decade of the twentieth century, the issue of authority was relocated for the Free Churches of Britain: from primary attention being devoted to biblical authority, there was now a search for new foundations for Christian understanding and practice, and in this situation the role of experience took on central importance.

Hugh Price Hughes

In the last two decades of the nineteenth century, Methodist theology changed radically. This movement was, in part, a product of the general cultural setting and the newly developing sensitivities of many theologians in different religious groups. But, in large measure, it resulted from the influence of one man – Hugh Price Hughes (1847–1902). Hughes was remarkable in many ways. Having come from a strong Methodist evangelical background, with a grandfather who was a Welsh Methodist preacher, he never forgot or turned from this heritage. At the same time, he was captured by a new vision of the relation of Christian faith to its social setting and, under its compulsion, he set the mission of his church upon a new course. As Christians, he maintained, we should never 'think of ourselves apart from Christ [or] think of ourselves apart from mankind'.[3]

Forward Movement

Hughes's was a radical voice [42], speaking both through his impassioned preaching and through the *Methodist Times*, a periodical which he established in 1884 and which became the conveyor of his thought. Through this publication Hughes took on the entire range of social issues: education, temperance, labour, peace and economic life. Fired by a fierce social conscience, Hughes insisted that his church should be a moral participant in the life of the nation and, on that fundamental conviction, he inaugurated a crusade under the title 'The Forward Movement'.

Nonconformist conscience

As a concrete embodiment of his understanding of Christian commitment he organized, in 1887, a new-style Methodist church, the West London Mission. But he was also ecumenical, and he called on all of the Free Churches, that is, the non-established Protestant churches, to band together to express their moral-social convictions. By using the notion of the 'nonconformist conscience', he tried to indicate that these churches could and should speak with one voice in the political affairs of the nation.

---

42. There was one man in Methodism in whom the holiness tradition and social concern were fused. Hugh Price Hughes came into Christian discipleship through the witness of the holiness of a Cornish fisherman. In the early part of his ministry he was actively associated with the Holiness Conventions lead by Pearsall Smith, and from first to last he was a zealous evangelist. In fact he combined evangelical zeal and political sensitivity to a high degree. He was a radical holiness man, if ever there was one.

Source: William Strawson, 'Methodist Theology 1850–1930' in Rupert Davies, A. Raymond George and Gordon Rupp (eds), *A History of Methodist Church in Great Britain*, vol. 3, Epworth Press 1983, p. 229.

Theological style

In several ways Hughes' style of theology represents a return to the Wesleys' practical approach. He begins with human experience, now broadened beyond immediate, direct relationship with Jesus Christ to include engagement with the social order, and interprets the gospel from that inclusive perspective. The interaction between practice and reflection is so tight that each draws from and shapes the other: thought provokes action, action provokes thought. Theology is not developed independently of concrete involvement in actual life experience.

Hugh Price Hughes makes no attempt to tackle, formally and directly, the intellectual challenges of the day or to cover the standard topics in a theological encyclopaedia. He deals, instead, with issues that force themselves upon a believer through experience of both Christ's redemption and societal needs. For

Hughes, theology involves practical involvement and practical involvement informs theology. Theology is thus addressed to all those attempting to live committed lives as Christian disciples, and it is intended to underwrite, deepen and enrich their commitment.

The phrase 'nonconformist conscience' became a by-word for the basis on which Christians not belonging to the established church could speak to their society. It made clear that, in a class-structured society, those outside the privileged positions had a special perspective, a vantage point from which they could judge the moral forms of the cultural and social setting.

Social renovation

Methodists, from the beginning, came from a broad spectrum of British society. Some Methodist bodies, such as the Primitive Methodists, the Methodist New Connexion and the Bible Christians, were strongest among labourers, miners, and all who carried the heavy toil of the nation. The Wesleyan Methodists tended to be found among small trades people, the aspiring class outside the establishment. In the first century of British Methodism there was an endorsement of the *status quo*, that is, there was respect for and acceptance of the existing structures of society. People were chiefly ambitious to find and utilize their own place. There was little direct challenge to the orders of society. But now, in the name of conscience, Hugh Price Hughes raised a challenge, intending not a revolution but a thorough renovation of dominant values and practices.

Hughes retained the revivalistic and evangelistic spirit which he inherited from his Methodist background. Indeed, it was this spirit that forged his continuing effort to win commitment to Jesus Christ and to strengthen commitment to the moral ordering of public life. Personal trust in a personal saviour was basic, and this he always asserted. But he was equally convinced that God's redemption, God's kingdom, must be extended to the whole life of people and societies. His own voice was clear and strong, and with great vigour he entered the public arena by endorsing, opposing, speaking and organizing [43].

> **43.** What we want above everything is a few Christ-like Christians. I say 'a few', because it is unreasonable to hope for very many at once . . . John Wesley expressed the same great truth in memorable words when he said, 'Ten true Christians would change the face of England.' He meant ten thorough-going Christians, ten Christ-like Christians, ten men or women animated by the Christian 'extra'. Will you be one of the ten?
>
> *Source*: Hugh Price Hughes, *Ethical Christianity*, Hodder and Stoughton 1892, p. 15.

Hughes did not think of himself as a theologian, certainly not as a theologian in the style of Watson or Pope. He was neither as intellectually disciplined as them nor as interested in precise differences among theological positions. He did not find value in discussion of abstract ideas. Rather, his attention was focussed upon activity; he was interested in the transformation of human life. 'Christianity does not say to us, "Sit and be convinced", but "Arise and walk".'[4]

Liberalizing Methodist theology

The theological scene among Protestants was changing as the nineteenth century closed. There was a renewed interest in 'the Fatherhood of God and the brotherhood of man', as Adolf von Harnack expressed the essence of Christianity. This theme became the identifying phrase of Protestant liberalism, which was an intense effort to grapple with dominant concepts in Western culture, such as historical consciousness, evolution and social Darwinianism, Idealistic philosophy and its challengers, and human kinship. The presiding theological category was 'the Kingdom of God', a phrase which captured both the primacy of God and the gathering of all creation under his sovereignty. Hughes shared this vision, as he put it, of 'The Fatherhood of God and the Kingdom of God'.[5]

Against this background, he welcomed the histor-ical study of scripture, the extension of interest into the general social arena and the necessary interrelation of theology and ethics, of Christian thought and social action. Maldwyn Edwards says that Hughes' work, and specifically the founding of the *Methodist Times*, 'is in fact a convenient date for marking the beginning of a dominant Liberalism within the Methodist Church'.[6]

Under this banner Hughes reminded his hearers of their daily prayer: 'Thy Kingdom come'. He spoke of religious life being lived in involvement with the present work-a-day world, not in monastic separation or other-wordliness. He encouraged Christians to seize this day for the work of love. He also addressed the questions of racism, militarism, the role and status of women, irresponsible wealth, the ranking of classes, the opium trade and the torture of animals. His concerns were wide and heralded the ethical issues which still face us [44].

> **44.** . . . in nearly every instance in which we find Jesus Christ face to face with the multitude the Evangelists tell us that He was 'moved with compassion' . . . The masses of suffering poor . . . a young man seeing his wife and children dying under his eyes . . . those poor girls in London, who are making a living – or, as Miss Rye rightly names it, 'a starving' . . . There are only two alternatives before us to-day – Christianity or revolution.
>
> *Source*: Hugh Price Hughes, *Social Christianity*, Hodder and Stoughton 1890, pp. 4, 5, 11, 15.

Preserving theological balance

At the same time he kept these current social interests in balance with more traditional themes. In *Essential Christianity*, for example, he argues that the response to Jesus Christ carries spiritual blessings and keeps the believer's eye on eternity, while also carrying responsibilities for service through self-giving to others. He concludes, 'Let us submit to Christ, let us yield ourselves to Him in all simplicity and heartiness; let us permit Him to do what He will in us, and with us, and through us.'[7]

His wife, Mary Katherine Howard Hughes, organized a religious order for women, a 'sisterhood', modelled on the ancient order of deacons and named 'Sisters of the People'. This was an affirmation of the role and contribution of women and was another expression of Hughes' openness to new times and to changing social roles. Mrs Hughes stressed that women were to develop all of their talents and, through the 'sisters', provided opportunity for leadership in service.

Achievement

With such an incandescence as Hughes the question is, of course: Is this an isolated flash or will it ignite a flame that spreads? In the case of Hugh Price Hughes, there can be no doubt of its continuing effect. He signals a new sense of mission; he does not establish a school of followers but he speaks for what will follow. Methodist theological leadership in Great Britain now faced the future with more open minds and more flexible attitudes, and willing to interpret the vitality of Christian faith in more comprehensive ways.

Transitions

Though aware of the dangers of superficiality, I want now to try to evoke, no matter how impressionistically, a sense of the immense and intense changes taking place in British society. The turn of the century witnessed the coronation of a new king but, since cultural changes do not take place on a calendar schedule [45], most of the dominant tendencies of the past several decades continued. Nonetheless, as the century progressed, changes altered societal and intellectual sensibilities.

The search for authority continued with increased urgency. Changes in the understanding of scriptural authority led to changes in understanding the authority of the creeds, and the publication in 1912 of a volume entitled *Foundations*[8] highlighted the fundamental challenge facing British culture. Outwardly, during the Edwardian decade the poise and purpose of Victoria's nation and empire continued undisturbed.

---

45. As the King went through its maze of apartments and corridors he came at last – and one can well believe with reluctance – into the private apartments of the Prince Consort. Nothing had been moved since Albert's death: the ink had hardened in the inkstands; intimate letters, yellow with age, lay just as he had left them; chairs, the desk, the carpets seemed to have been waiting for forty years for Albert to return. In one corner stood the organ upon which he had played to Mendelssohn, but it was perished and voiceless. Had the King ever penetrated these rooms before, for some awful interview with that formidable parent? We do not know. He ordered everything to be packed up and put away with care. And then the electrician, the plumber, the cleaner and the Twentieth Century came in.

Source: George Dangerfield, *Victoria's Heir*, New York 1942, p. 537.

But underneath there were rumbles of change [46], and a new Parliament in 1906 embodied a political shift which would make its impact felt through the twentieth century.

---

46. Personal memories of Edward VII have transferred to it [the decade] something of the king's own character and atmosphere. Men think of the decade as one of calm and contentment, of pomp and luxury, of assured wealth and unchallenged order. Court splendours apart, it was none of these things. It was an era of growth and strain, of idealism and reaction, of swelling changes and seething unrest. At home, politics had never been so bitter; abroad, the clouds were massing for Armageddon.

Source: Sir Robert Ensor, *England 1870–1914*, Clarendon Press 1936, p. 421.

The twentieth century: background to ecclesiastical and theological developments

Throughout the twentieth century the relation of the church to the state has been changing and there have been times of intense strain. A decline in church membership and participation has complicated the situation, and no simple analyses or explanations are possible. But perhaps a brief description of the cultural and social situation can set a general background for both ecclesiastical and theological developments.

In the year 1910 changes already taking place were focussed and portents of what was to come appeared. On 6 May King Edward died. Virginia Woolf expressed her conviction about the time: 'On or about December 1910 human character changed . . . All human relations have shifted – those between masters and servants, husbands and wives, parents and children. And when human relations change there is at the same time a change in religion, conduct, politics and literature.'[9] As extravagant as that claim may seem, there were undoubtedly radical changes evident in the world of art, and Sir Herbert Read stated boldly, 'The modern period in British art may be said to date from the year 1910 . . .'[10] Moreover, C. M. Bowra locates the beginning of a new poetic style in this year.[11] Again, Bertrand Russell and Alfred North Whitehead published *Principia Mathematica*, which related mathematics to logic and language to both in a new way, and Idealistic philosophy was under sharp attack from G. E. Moore and Russell. Inevitably, theology was drawn into the maelstrom of change.

World War I and its aftermath

The year 1910, then, pointed ahead, and decades of political and nationalistic development culminated in World War I [47], always called 'the Great War' by British people. Its causes were complex and its impact decisive. Rudyard Kipling had already voiced a warning in his poem 'Recessional':

> Far-called, our navies melt away –
>   On dunes and headland sinks the fire –
> Lo, all our pomp of yesterday
>   Is one with Ninevah and Tyre!
> Judge of all Nations, spare us yet,
>   Lest we forget – lest we forget.

The war itself exacted a terrible price in human life, in human suffering, in shifts of values, in attitudes

> **47.** Nietzsche recognized the waning of religion as a primary force in people's lives and flung his challenge in these words: 'God is dead!' He would have substituted Superman, but ordinary people substituted patriotism. As faith in God retreated before the advance of science, love of country began to fill the empty spaces in the heart. Nationalism absorbed the strength once belonging to religion. Where people formerly fought for religion now they would presumably do no less for its successor. A sense of gathering conflict filled the air.
>
> *Source*: Barbara Tuchman, *The Proud Tower*, New York 1962, p. 250.

toward life. Poets and novelists, politicians and theologians attempted to assess the ravages of the conflict. And theology in Great Britain intensely explored the meaning of evil and the power of evil destructiveness in human life [48].

> **48.** . . . war was ever a kind of apocalyptic and its carelessness of our civilization and all its belongings and its reckless disregard of life and all its securities. Ancient judgments vanish like ancient treasures, and ideas men had thought eternal are discovered to be only the fashion of a departing time. And when this war is over a new age will be upon us also, a better or worse according as we bear ourselves in the material and the spiritual conflict, but certainly another age, and those of us who are not prepared to reconsider all our judgments and help to build a new heaven and a new earth will not be able to retain the old, but will only wander in the new time as shadowy ghosts of a vanished past.
>
> *Source*: John Oman, *The War and Its Issues*, Cambridge University Press 1915, pp. 4–5.

The war both quickened changes already in the making and brought new changes of its own making. Hope for a new world order, immediate affirmation that this was the war to end all wars, anticipation of a new society of greater equality and social cohesion was met with some success in the establishment of women's suffrage and the expressions of labour organization. Nevertheless, the decades between the two World Wars were a time of frustrated hopes and deep-seated social unrest.

The war had washed away the past at a terrible cost, and now the nation turned and faced a new present and future walking upon new ground. The war was a trench dug between the past and the present, a wound standing in the middle of no-man's-land, and most people seemed willing to forget and not attempt to move back across the forbidding terrain. People were now in new territory. They were in a new present, occupiers of a new place, inhabitants of a new age [49].

---

49. After the war men must face again the old questions which perplexed them before, but which the strain of the crisis drove from mind . . . The traditional theology will be again seen to be plainly inadequate to express the truth of religion as they must need perceive it.

Source: H. H. Henson, 'The Church After the War' in *The Faith and The War*, F. J. Foakes-Jackson (ed), London 1915, p. 256.

But what was this new age? The period between the wars was a time of increasing secularism in British life. In 1929 Arnold Bennett in *Affirmations* claimed that the intelligentsia is uninterested in God and that 'the affair is over and done with'.[12] The sense is extreme, but Bennett, as a novelist, often reflected the mood of the time. The after-shock of readjustment brought three words to the fore, 'reconstruction, restoration, recovery'.[13]

Peace and quiet were difficult to achieve. On 15 November 1922 there was a national election, followed by two more general elections in less than two years (26 December 1923, 29 October 1924). The political changes reflected deep upheavals in the life of the nation. Specifically, there was the growing power of socialism, in the form of the Labour Party; and Stanley Baldwin and Ramsay MacDonald succeeded David Lloyd George as the political leaders of the country. In 1926 there was a General Strike which

reflected wrenching economic strife. The era was tumultuous.

Looking back, it may be that the single most important change made after the war was the new status of women. The Representation of the People act of 1918 gave the vote to all adult men and to all women over thirty years of age. By 1928 there were fifteen million women voters compared to thirteen and a half million men.[14]

Lord Haldane indicated the difference he saw in the social and religious setting: 'Today the external conditions of life in civilized communities differ more from those of 1830 than the conditions of 1830 from those of Noah's flood.'[15] The church was plainly face to face with a secular world, a world indifferent to Christian claims; and W. H. Auden asked:

What do you think about England,
This country of ours where nobody is well?[16]

The challenge of the scientific ethos

Chief among the changes in general cultural sensibilities was the increasing dominance of a scientific ethos. In the introduction to *Foundations*, B. H. Streeter commented on 'The Modern Situation'. The situation was modern precisely because contemporary persons had to deal with the critical study of scripture, the problems of industrial urban life and the expansion of confidence of scientific knowledge. So thorough had been the recent changes, he contended, that the resulting insecurity had reached the foundations not only of the now forsaken Victorian assumptions but of the Christian religion itself[17] [50].

Twentieth-century Great Britain, like Western culture generally, has been dominated by a generalized scientific ethos. The origin and development of this perspective is too complex to specify in detail or with exactness. But, from the eighteenth century, the progress of scientific theory and its application developed with inexorable force; by the twentieth century, the 'scientific paradigm' of how one knows was a general possession of most persons. There has been not only an intellectual but a moral affirmation

50. Ford, we are twelve; oh, make us one,
    Like drops within the Social River;
  Oh, make us now together run
    As swiftly as thy shining Flivver . . .

  Come, Greater Being, Social Friend,
    Annihilating Twelve-in-one!
  We long to die, for when we end,
    Our larger life has but begun . . .

  Feel how the Greater Being comes!
    Rejoice and, in rejoicing, die!
  Melt in the music of the drums!
    For I am you and you are I.

Source: Aldous Huxley, *Brave New World*, Chatto 1932;
Penguin Books 1955, p. 71.

---

of the scientific approach. The work of the scientist is taken to possess a character of care and honesty, an openness to new evidence, a willingness to make only limited claims, and a rigorous industry in the search for relevant data. There is also an undeniable achievement through scientifically based discovery and technology, and it may be that slow but thorough practical efforts were among the most persuasive aspects of the perceptual-conceptual transformation. The practice of medicine, availability of electricity, means of transportation, discovery of radio and other practical supports of life were convincing.

Theology and the scientific ethos

For theology both the methodological foundations and the final achievements of science have been important. Scientific advances have constituted a direct challenge. Positively, theology throughout the century has struggled with the possibility of a scientific method for its own work. Negatively, theology has had to contend with indifference to its claims and with scepticism about the validity of its assumptions and conclusions.

Philosophical and other challenges

The most direct philosophical challenge to theology was issued by A. J. Ayer in his book *Language, Truth and Logic* (1936) which set the primary intellectual agenda for theology for several decades. In this book, Ayer argued that there are only two valid forms of knowledge: that which is empirically verified and that which is tautological or definitional. By this criterion, metaphysics, theology and ethics are all, strictly speaking, nonsense. That is, they have no status as knowledge. The dismissal was direct and theologians had to respond. Epistemology became the subject matter of philosophical theology.

The era between the wars witnessed little in the way of religious revival. In fact, Robert Graves and Alan Hodge deal with the Christian faith in only a few sentences in their book *The Long Weekend*, a social history of the era. Church attendance continued to decline; and, as though to fill the void, other movements gained notoriety if not general support [51]. From the East came Indian religions, both Hindu and

---

51.   CREED OF ST EUTHANASIA

(Commonly called the Athenaeum Creed)

I believe in Man. Maker of himself and Investor of all
  Science.
  And in Myself, his Manifestation, and Captain of my
    Psyche;
  and that I should not suffer anything painful or
    unpleasant.

And in a vague Evolving Deity, the future-begotten Child
  of Man; conceived by the
  Spirit of progress, born of Emergent Variants; who
    shall kick down the ladder by
  which he rose and tell history to go to hell;

Who shall some day take off from earth and be jet-
  propelled into the heavens; and sit
  exalted above all worlds, Man the Master Al-
    mighty . . .

Source: Dorothy L. Sayers, *Christian Letters to a Post-
Christian World*, Grand Rapids 1969, p. 11.

Yoga, and Chinese philosophy. Prominent persons espoused various forms of oriental religion: C. E. M. Joad called for the recognition of the philosophy of S. Radhakrishnan and I. A. Richards wrote a book on Mencius. There were spiritualistic and Theosophic groups which gained converts, and from domestic environs came the Oxford Group Movement (Buchmanites or Moral Rearmament). Yet this was not the whole story, for traditional Christianity continued to be a significant, if more subdued, part of the cultural and social scene.

World War II

In less than a quarter of a century there was another major war. World War I had decimated the brightest and best of young British manhood; so much so that George Steiner has claimed that there was a change in the gene-pool. World War II was even more devastating. The air raids, the total mobilization, the displacement of people, the cost in physical and psychological energy took enormous toll. The nation which was in constant change experienced an intensification of change and a reordering of life.

It appeared, in fact, that the historic supports of Christian faith were all giving way. Traditionally, the legs of the stool of Christian confidence had been scripture, creeds and reason, and each was now undermined in turn. By the end of the nineteenth century, scriptural authority was undergoing radical reassessment. Early in the twentieth century, the questioning moved to matters of creedal affirmation, such as the Virgin Birth. But, since British Idealism was, in many ways, a religious philosophy, reason at first seemed secure. Then, as we have seen, A. J. Ayer relegated theological, moral and metaphysical statements to the category of 'non-sense' and reason, as confidently espoused by Idealism, became in uncertain support. Theology needed to formulate new bases for its endeavours.

During the interwar period and especially after William Temple's major work, *Nature, Man and God* (1934), non-Anglican scholars produced much of the significant theological work: such leaders were John Oman and H. H. Farmer in theology and C. H. Dodd and T. W. Manson in New Testament studies. Methodists also made important contributions through such figures as Vincent Taylor, William F. Lofthouse, J. Alexander Findlay and Wilbert F. Howard.

Two decades after the end of the Great War, Europe was once again in an all out conflict. Nations, which had paid dearly in human and material destruction in World War I, were once again involved in a life and death struggle. The cost for Great Britain was enormous. Enemy bombing caused widespread devastation, and the physical and emotional life of the civilian population, which was directly targeted, was under the severest pressure. Only the will to survive kept the nation alive. When one reads the chronicles, a sense of awe and admiration is the only appropriate response to the resourcefulness and determination of the British people.

In 1944, amid the ravages of war, Leslie D. Weatherhead preached five sermons at City Temple which were printed together under the title *The Will of God*. It was a tract for the times and eventually sold almost one million copies. In these sermons Weatherhead struggled with the issue of theodicy, of the waste of war, and Christian affirmation of God's love. He made three distinctions: God's intentional will – God's original, ideal plan; God's circumstantial will – God's will in concrete, historical circumstances; and God's ultimate will – God's final realization of divine purpose. Using these categories he attempted to root God's intention in love, to understand the destruction caused by human freedom and to affirm the ultimate fulfilment of God's providence. The dynamic of the interpretation evoked response and helped many people deal with the reality of loss and establish hope for renewal.

Another important development by the fourth decade was the theological writing of authors of imaginative literature, namely such persons as C. S. Lewis, Charles Williams and Dorothy Sayers. A. J. Ayer had set the debate and professional theologians were struggling with issues of empirical verification, the epistemological basis of theological claims, and ethics as more than emotive expression.

The immediate precedent for literary figures serving theological interpretation was the work of T. S. Eliot in the 1920s. After describing the spiritual wasteland of contemporary life and the hollow condition – a condition displayed in banal insensitivity and shallowness of human relationships – of people living there, Eliot turned with his poem 'Ash Wednesday' (1930) to the theme of God's grace. Eliot set the path by naming the new gods who were being worshipped and the false structuring of human life, then confronting this crushing modernity with a strong affirmation of inherited Christian doctrine. Others soon followed his lead.

Especially in the decades of the 1940s and 1950s, while academic theologians contended with the establishing of viable bases for their claims, authors such as Lewis, Williams and Sayers moved to another literary genre, imaginative literature, and created worlds where meaningful, decisive and hopeful action could take place. They thus offered a creative alternative to scientifically restricted technological culture. Lewis and Sayers also wrote straightforward theological statements [52], but it was their plays and novels that most powerfully conveyed Christian affirmation, a sense of confidence, and the power of commitment.

For many readers, this genre provided clearer access to theological understandings than did traditional types of theological treatise and a chance to move along a narrative path towards a new world of redemption.

---

52. The right faith is, that we believe that Jesus Christ is God *and* Man. Perfect God and perfect Man, of a reasonable soul and human flesh subsisting. Who although He be God and Man, yet is He not two, but one Christ. There is the essential doctrine, of which the whole elaborate structure of Christian faith and morals is only the logical consequence.

Source: Dorothy L. Sayers, *Creed or Chaos?*, New York 1949, p. 7.

In general, academic British theology awaited a more congenial philosophical context. Special attention was given to the later philosophy of Ludwig Wittgenstein, to new accommodations of religion and science or to post-Enlightenment developments. And what of Methodist theology? Gordon Wakefield has an assessment: 'It could be argued that Methodism's greatest failure since Union has been theological, an inability to interpret the Divine presence and activity in the world, through the ways of the gospel. Some good things have been and are being said, but we have been too much the victims of pragmatism, too absorbed in administration and in preparing documents Conference will approve, to foster the contemplative vocation either for scholarship or prayer.'[18]

In this chapter, we have attempted to indicate some of the social and cultural transitions which have characterized twentieth-century British life. Methodism has lived within this context and has necessarily been deeply affected by these societal changes. Nevertheless, the context has remained general; there is no point-to-point relation of Methodist theological developments to specific changes. In basic ways, Methodism has continued to reflect intellectual interests peculiar to its own history and inherited concerns. Perhaps in its reach for union with the Church of England the Methodist Church has sought greater involvement in dominant cultural developments; but, for the most part, Methodism has remained distinguishable by the continuation of issues nurtured within its own ecclesiastical life. These continuing themes we shall now explore.

For discussion

1. Examine the main characteristics of Hugh Price Hughes' work. Which of them is still relevant today?
2. As early as 1910, a number of influences had begun to change British society. Which of them has affected Methodism most?
3. Has Methodism, indeed have any of us as indivi-

duals, come to terms with the traumas, psychological, spiritual and intellectual, produced by two World Wars?

4. The chapter highlights the contributions of writers like Dorothy L. Sayers, T. S. Eliot, C. S. Lewis and Charles Williams to theological literature. Do they have continuing value?

5. How do you react to Gordon Wakefield's suggestion that 'it could be argued that Methodism's greatest failure since Union has been theological'?

5

Scripture, Experience, Atonement

So far in this book we have proceeded chronologically, discussing theologians and theological issues as they have appeared on the historical scene. In this chapter, still working chronologically, we look at three major pre-occupations of twentieth-century British Methodist theology.

Because the contributors to the discussion were Methodists, the whole range of issues was of some interest and importance to all of them. As a result, there is a criss-crossing of issues and interpreters. Several major figures made contributions on more than one issue, and we will therefore try to describe a web of interaction, a process of lateral as well as forward movement.

We begin with the place of scripture, move to the emphasis on religious experience, and conclude with ways in which the atonement has been understood.

Scripture

It may reasonably be claimed that British Methodism has made its major contribution to ecumenical Christianity through its biblical scholarship. Such a claim, moreover, is hardly surprising, granted that, from the beginning, Methodism has seen itself as biblically based and given special attention to Bible study.

John Wesley initiated this theological commitment. In the famous preface to the *Forty-four Sermons*, he describes himself as 'a man of one book' and goes on to indicate his own method of studying scripture. Both his sermons and his brother's hymns, furthermore,

vividly illustrate a profound dependence upon the Bible; and the importance he attached to biblical study among Methodists may be judged from his preparation of *Notes* on the Old and New Testaments and his effort to make use of the best commentaries of his time.

It is entirely in keeping, therefore, that Adam Clarke's commentary on the entire Bible should be a by-product of his own scripture study, undertaken to inform his preaching. Equally, the fact that the primacy of scripture was constantly re-affirmed throughout the nineteenth century, being made utterly explicit in the theology of Richard Watson and William Burt Pope, is scarcely unexpected.

By the late nineteenth century, however, a new era was entered and new attitudes emerge. The change did not concern the primacy and authority of scripture so much as its nature and interpretation. Methodist scholars, in fact, made important contributions to the study of New Testament Greek and other relevant languages, and to the interpretation of the New Testament itself.

As a result, there was a shift in the understanding of scripture: from fully inspired, infallible word (the view of Watson and Pope) to a set of documents inspired by God, witnessing to Jesus Christ and used by the Holy Spirit (the position which became representative among Methodists). The change was not the result of a set battle about hermeneutical principles. Rather, it developed slowly through careful textual work, and new methods of interpretation emerged as the most appropriate ways of respecting and understanding the New Testament documents.

The Moultons

W. F. Moulton (1829–1898) was extremely important because of his translation and excellent annotation of Winer's *Grammar of New Testament Greek*. Such careful grammatical work led to fine exegesis of the Gospel of John and the book of Hebrews. He also wrote *The History of the English Bible*, which helped prepare the path for future evaluations of the nature and significance of the scriptures.

If possible, a son out-shone his father, for James Hope Moulton (1865–1917) continued the meticulous linguistic work with *A Grammar of New Testament Greek* and, in doing so, established an international reputation. His insistence that biblical Greek was *koine* or the vernacular Greek of daily life was particularly significant. Both of the Moultons were Methodist ministers, and their scholarship was twinned with a strong affirmation of the basic Methodist convictions about conversion, Christian experience and sanctification.

Wilbert F. Howard

Wilbert F. Howard (1880–1952) continued this line of study as he completed the second volume of J. H. Moulton's *Prolegomena*. He went on, however, to become a major interpreter of Johannine literature and served both his scholarly colleagues and, as he intended, his fellow preachers, lay and ordained, in their interpretation of these writings. His two books *The Fourth Gospel in Recent Criticism and Interpretation* (1931) and *Christianity According to St John* (1943) represent these two dimensions of his work. Again, following in the path of W. F. Moulton, he wrote *The Romance of New Testament Scholarship* [53], using the biographies of significant scholars to win interest in New Testament studies. Commentaries on I and II Corinthians, Acts and the Gospel of John contributed to deeper understanding of these texts, not least in academic circles.

> 53. When we speak of the 'romance of New Testament scholarship', we think of the remarkable way in which, within the last century, the clues contained in these remains of early Christian writings have been followed up. The text of the apostolic writings is being slowly recovered. Lost books have been found, sometimes in the papyrus rolls and codices long buried in the sands of Egypt, sometimes in vellum books buried and forgotten in ancient monasteries or libraries and often concealed in a translation made centuries ago into some little-known language or dialect. The history of the Church is being rewritten as scholars read between the lines of the sacred writings, or recover the atmosphere of an age of which the records are scarce and fragmentary. Words, phrases, and allusions in the New Testament are charged with fresh significance, because the language and laws, the habits and customs, the private and the public life of a dead world have risen from the grave before our very eyes.
>
> *Source*: W. F. Howard, *The Romance of New Testament Scholarship*, Epworth Press 1949, p. 32.

Arthur S. Peake

The Primitive Methodist biblical scholar, Arthur S. Peake (1865–1929), was also outstanding. Peake, as much as any single person, helped make criticial study of the biblical text a part of Methodist biblical interpretation. A man of independent mind, yet loyal to his church, he was the first Methodist to hold a chair in biblical study in a major university in Great Britain (Manchester).

Methodism's search for unity was an important context for Peake's work. During the first third of the twentieth century, Methodist bodies seriously discussed the possibility of organizational unity, and in the Union finally accomplished in 1932 institutional issues were more easily resolved than doctrinal ones. John Kent, in discussing the preceding events, says, 'Institutional issues presented so little difficulty that the compromise arrived at in 1920 was hardly altered in succeeding years.'[1] The most disputed matters were doctrinal, especially those relating to church, ministry and sacraments and the role of scripture. Where scripture was concerned, many among non-Wesleyan Methodist groups were unwilling to take John Wesley's *Notes* as authoritative.

Peake, a layman and a teacher at the Primitive Methodist theological college in Manchester, was outspoken, saying that he would have preferred to omit any reference to the writings of John Wesley from the doctrinal statement of the united Methodist Church. To many, certainly, the new critical study of the Bible made Wesley's pre-critical interpretations seem obsolete, and one Primitive Methodist commentator wrote, 'Frankly, many of us *don't* believe what John Wesley believed.'[2] In 1919 the Wesleyan Conference adopted a resolution which said that the *Notes* and the forty-four sermons were 'not intended to impose a formal or speculative theology on our preachers'.[3] The final basis of Methodist union, having accepted this position, went on to affirm that the Holy Spirit would safeguard the development of doctrine in a faithful church and that it was fundamental to the spiritual freedom of a living church that it should interpret its own standards. John Kent comments that 'this mention of development was what the non-Wesleyan churches required to balance the implication that Wesley had set down the system of Evangelical truth once and for all'.[4]

The scope of Peake's biblical work was extremely broad. Following the example of Wesley and Clarke, he edited a *Commentary on the Bible* (1919) and, while he concentrated on Paul and Pauline literature, he also engaged in theological discussions and wrote commentaries on biblical books as wide-ranging as Job, Jeremiah, Colossians, Hebrews and Revelation. Peake's enthusiasm and enormous energy made him an active participant in church life and in the negotiations which led to the union of Methodist bodies in Great Britain. His biblical work was characterized by an incessant effort to deal with critical questions of an historical and textual nature, but this did not mean that he neglected the message of the texts. He both brought change and represented the change which he brought.

J. Alexander Findlay

Another significant person within this sequence of major biblical scholars was J. Alexander Findlay (1880–1961). Findlay, in contrast to many of his predecessors, concentrated more on the interpretation of the New Testament than on critical issues, as his major writings indicate: *Jesus As They Saw Him* (1919–20), *What Did Jesus Teach?* (1933), *Jesus and His Parables* (1939), and *The Way, The Truth, The Life* (1940). Findlay was an engaging teacher whose interpretations both reflected his era and contributed – for example, through his interest in the humanity of Jesus and the way in which God's revelation has come through a human life – to the agenda of his time.

Findlay's interpretations were sensitive and carefully wrought. The way in which he deals with the humanity of Jesus shows that he was aware of other interpretations, especially those being put forward by continental theologians like Karl Barth. The foundation of Findlay's position was the immanence of God and the basic goodness of human nature. He was aware of the erosion of innate goodness by sin, but for him there was a residual relationship of human beings with God, a relationship which required reawakening and reinforcing by the historical presence of Jesus [54]. Jesus both called forth recognition of this innate human potential and mediated the power of such a new relationship with God.

---

54. Perhaps only when we look into His face shall we really grasp the final truth which binds all life together – that this Jesus who lived with us and died for us is one with the God who is in everything. Prophets and poets have caught a glimpse of the shining of His robes as He passed by; they longed to see His face, and died without the sight, leaving behind them but a baffling suggestion of what they had seen . . . can He who has given us rest of soul, this Jesus in whose presence alone we have ever known what it was altogether to forget ourselves, altogether to find ourselves – can He be less than God? If He is not divine, then we have lost the master-key of life and death.

Source: J. Alexander Findlay, *Jesus, Human and Divine*, Epworth Press 1938, p. 20.

Three dominant themes of the era were paramount in Findlay's thought: the immanence of God, the possibility of presenting an authentic and full portrait of the human Jesus, and the centrality of human experience as the material factor in religious life. These themes run through Findlay's expositions of the relation of creation to redemption, of Jesus as the human person who evoked and enabled relationship with God, and of the intellectual and emotional conviction which that relationship supplied.

Confidence about the possibility of writing a biography of Jesus, of knowing both his activity and his self-consciousness, was strong. Among many British scholars of the first half of the twentieth century this conviction provided a strong drive to biblical study and fresh portraiture of Jesus. In addition, Findlay presented this historical Jesus in ways which were winsome and appealing.

To read Findlay is to be drawn into the presentation of a Jesus who, in life, death and resurrection, embodied the highest ideal of human life and the character of God. For him these two dimensions, thoroughly intertwined, conveyed the essential message of the New Testament.

Vincent Taylor

The final scholar we shall mention from this era is Vincent Taylor (1882–1968). Taylor, like the Moultons and Howard, always began with close textual study. He investigated the background to the Gospel of Luke in *Behind the Third Gospel: A Study of the Proto-Luke Hypothesis* (1926), and then undertook an exploration of the form-critical claims of contemporary German scholars. The form critics took the 'setting in the life' in which the New Testament was produced as of central importance – indeed, for them it provided the necessary background for interpretation. To explore this position required close, thorough textual analysis. With prodigious energy Taylor assessed these claims in *The Formation of the Gospel Tradition* (1933). These two books established Taylor's position among New Testament scholars and revealed his own cautious attitude towards interpre-

tive theories. Perhaps his most significant exegetical work was his commentary, *The Gospel according to St Mark* (1932).

Vincent Taylor also undertook studies in New Testament theology. They bore fruit, first, in a trilogy on the meaning of the atonement: *Jesus and His Sacrifice* (1937), *The Atonement in New Testament Teaching* (1940) and *Forgiveness and Reconciliation* (1946), to which we will return in our discussion of the atonement later in this chapter; and later in a trilogy on christology: *The Names of Jesus* (1953), *The Life and Ministry of Jesus* (1954), and *The Person of Christ in New Testament Teaching* (1958). All of these books are extended expositions of biblical materials.

What is evident, even from the brief treatment of these scholars, is the magnitude of the contribution of British Methodists to biblical study in the twentieth century. The fact that these studies were undertaken, their method of approach, and the biblical themes upon which they concentrated reflect strong sinews of the Methodist tradition. In John Wesley's theological quadrilateral, scripture was primary, and these distinguished scholars accepted this primacy, in theory and practice.

The important question is: how did these scholars affect Methodism's understanding of the use of scripture for theological interpretation? The basic answer seems to be that they broke the use of the Bible as proof texts or as a systematic handbook for theology but opened up its use as a resource and a guide. Scripture authority remained, and in some ways was strengthened, as the fundamental foundation of Christian understanding. But scripture was now understood to be in dynamic dialogue – both affirmatively and critically – with traditional and current interpretations.

To claim that scripture is the primary source of theology is not to conclude the discussion; it is, rather, to open it. For scripture always stands in relation to an interpretive tradition and an historical setting. The Holy Spirit becomes the crucial agent in bringing the unique biblical past into living relation with the changing and challenging present. Hence to make scripture primary is to affirm the role of the Holy Spirit as interpreter. And to recognize an interpretive tradition is to emphasize the significance of a community which shapes, forms, criticizes and enhances biblical interpretation.

These biblical scholars were important in Methodism because they guided its tradition into this new understanding and new appreciation of scripture.

Experience

In the early years of the twentieth century the theme of 'experience' was dominant in British Methodist theology. From the beginning, of course, Methodists have been interested in Christian experience: John Wesley had spoken of a heart-warming; Methodists were called enthusiasts; and there had been much concern with conversion, maturation and holiness. Indeed, the whole cast of Methodist theology as 'practical' had made experience a central issue. But now it was theologically crucial as never before.

The term 'experience' is extremely difficult to define, since it is used quite differently by different writers [55]. Consequently, it is necessary to be especially careful when referring to Methodism as experientially based.

> 55. I intend to disobey that excellent rule which bids us always define our terms at the beginning. For one thing, there are no two words in language harder to define than religion and experience; for another, to define religious experience would help no one unacquainted with it to understand it; since, just as no definition of beauty would explain beauty to any one who had not experienced it, no definition of religious experience will make that term clear to those who do not share it.
>
> *Source*: Eric S. Waterhouse, 'The Methodist Appeal to Experience', London n.d., *c.* 1926.

Definitions

For Wesley, for instance, experience means primarily personal relationship with Jesus Christ as mediated by the Holy Spirit. The event of Jesus Christ is not derived from experience, it is given to experience as a shaping, vitalizing, commanding sanction for life [56]. By the late nineteenth century, in contrast, Methodism moved to a more subjective approach, according to which experience is the source of data for interpretation. There is, it was held, a vague referential object to which experience 'points', and the variety of religious traditions has arisen from different attempts to identify and understand it. In the earlier era, experience was receptive and mediatorial; in the latter period, it was originating and productive. Hence, in order to be theologically useful, the meaning of experience had to be concretely specified.

> 56. First of all, then, Wesley and the early Methodists grounded religion and theology in the fact of experience. This was a revolution in theological practice, for it was the revolutionary application to theology of what is really scientific method.
>
> *Source*: Henry Bett, *The Spirit of Methodism*, Epworth Press 1937, p. 131.

By the turn of the twentieth century, then, 'experience' was the dominant theme in English-speaking theology both in Great Britain and North America. There were several reasons for this. First, there was a general and new insistence on rooting Christian interpretation in human experience. In other words, the period witnessed a decisive shift in the focus of concentration, from received texts and creeds to actual, historical human existence. This was, in part, a response to the dominant scientific assumption: namely, that human experience provides data for scientific investigation, description and interpretation. Theologies that were concentrating on the ways in which the immanent God acts in human history, rather than emphasizing the irruptive, transcendent action of God, were another factor. For them, the permeative presence of God in human experience was the presupposition, and scientific exploration became the method of study.

Experience and psychology

Again, there was a growing interest in psychology, pre-occupation with human experience giving rise to attention to its many dimensions. The fountainhead of this interest was William James' *Varieties of Religious Experience* (1902), a classic study which set the agenda for an era. In addition, the interest in religious experience was enlarged by a new awareness of non-Christian experience – as recorded, for example, in J. G. Frazer's *The Golden Bough*. Frazer collected evidence of a vast range of religious experiences, from the primitive to the contemporary. As a result, human religious experiences were studied in a comparative fashion in order to deepen understanding of other religions as well as Christianity.

For Methodism, general interest in religious experience, as we have seen, matched an element in their own tradition and gave impetus to attempts to understand it better. Methodist theologians, in fact, turned their attention to questions relating to religious experience [57], and did so with enthusiasm.

---

57. William James and others, twenty-five years or more ago, drew attention to the tremendous argument that could be based on religious experience. At the same time the scientific study of religion was demonstrating the existence of religion as a factor of first-rate importance in the social life of humanity from the earliest days downward. After that, it was no longer possible to regard religion as a system of superstitions foisted on the people be priestcraft. Religion is acknowledged now as a universal expression of the human spirit, and a factor of the utmost historical, psychological, and sociological importance. The genuinely human character of religion, therefore, is recognized by every thinker today. What is questioned is not that, it is its divine character.

Source: Eric S. Waterhouse, 'The Methodist Appeal to Experience', London n.d., *c.* 1926, p. 4.

A theology of experience

In his article 'Methodist Theology, 1850–1950', William Strawson comments, 'The idea that Methodist theology is a "theology of experience" . . . is basically true of the systematic theology of Methodism from 1900–1932. This theology is centered on the experience of salvation; God is thought of mainly in terms of His redeeming activity and all other doctrines are subservient to this evangelical concern.'[5]

To illustrate this development, several books which concentrated on experience as a point of theological leverage can be mentioned. John G. Tasker in *Spiritual Religion: A Study of the Relation of Facts to Faith* (London 1901) develops a scientific approach to the knowledge of God, beginning with a type of natural theology which seeks God as revealed in nature and in human nature. He then goes on to insist on the necessity of God's revelation in Jesus Christ if persons are to find the truest and most adequate understanding of God. The book, in short, expresses a mediating position between a dogmatic theology derived from scripture and the creeds and a theology grounded solely in the exploration of human experience.

Frederick W. Platt in *Immanence and Christian Thought: Implications and Suggestions* (London 1915) makes fully evident the relation of the theological emphasis upon immanence with the investigation of religious experience. One finds the same emphasis in Maldwyn Hughes' theology, culminating in *Christian Foundations: An Introduction to Christian Doctrine* (London 1927). And even more explicit is the work of George Jackson, *The Fact of Conversion* (London 1908), which utilizes psychology as the medium for understanding religious experience.

These interests can also be found in the work of John Scott Lidgett (to whom we shall return later in this chapter) and in the writing of C. Ryder Smith, particularly in his book *The Christian Experience: A Study in the Theology of Fellowship* (London 1926). While Smith went on to publish a series of books which deal with major biblical concepts, he was in intention a theologian working with data drawn from concrete human experience. Psychology was the science which he used, and in this he reflected the theological climate of his age.

Typical of Methodist affirmation of experience as

the basis of Christian theology was H. Maldwyn Hughes' *The Theology of Experience* (London 1915). Hughes begins with religious experience as a universal phenomenon, then concentrates on Christian experience which, he insists, is always informed by the historical revelation in Jesus [58]. Hughes writes, 'Christian experience is unique and pre-eminent because of the range of its vision, the depth of its transforming power, and the authority of its conviction of the truth of its contents . . .'[6]

58. Christian experience, then, does not depend for its authority merely on the self-attestation of states of consciousness, but on an objective historical revelation, the truth of which is confirmed by the response which it awakens, and the fruit which it produces, as well as by the application of the ordinary canons of history.

Source: H. Maldwyn Hughes, *The Theology of Experience*, Epworth Press 1915, p. 31.

According to this approach, theology formulates doctrine by interpreting the facts of Christianity's historical revelation and the experience of its adherents; and its work must be tested by scientific, philosophical, historical and literary criticism in order to craft a statement applicable to a particular era.[7] Both experience and interpretation of experience undergo 'creative evolution', and fresh experience of the historical revelation in Jesus Christ provides opportunity for fresh theological understanding.

Religious experience in the Methodist tradition is closely tied to conversion and the transformation of human life, and thus to study experience is a mode of practical theology, closely related to the doctrine of the atonement. Talk of experience and talk of atonement are mutually dependent, and therefore the interpretations of atonement, to which we turn, extend the meaning of Christian experience.

Atonement

The question of how God has acted to effect reconciliation between persons and God and to establish a new life in Christ has been a vital issue throughout the history of British Methodism.

From John Wesley to Richard Watson, the theme of Jesus' substitutionary death as a means of satisfying the justice of God was central in Methodist theology, as it was in the Reformation theology of that period. God in Christ, it was affirmed, has taken the place of sinful human beings and has brought about a reconciliation through his death on the cross. In effecting a reconciliation between God and human beings Jesus Christ has satisfied the honour and justice of God and the human need for forgiveness.

By mid-nineteenth century, as we shall see, other theories had appeared on the British scene. William Burt Pope, however, was reluctant to rely on any single theory to interpret the atonement. Its meaning, he held, could more adequately be portrayed by using the full range of concepts which had come down in Christian tradition.

After Pope, though Methodist interest in the atonement continued, most interpreters thought any effort to hold all of the theories together could confuse the issue and fail to yield a central emphasis. Attempts to specify the ways in which the atonement actually changed human life constitute a significant development. Previously, theologians tended to concentrate on the difference the atonement made to God; now attention was focussed upon the difference it made to human beings.

John Scott Lidgett

The major Methodist figure was John Scott Lidgett (1854–1953). Lidgett was a remarkable man. He has been called 'the greatest Methodist since John Wesley', and such high praise reflects the respect he enjoyed. He was deeply rooted in his evangelical heritage and always spoke as a representative of that tradition. But he was also fully aware of the intellectual movements of his time and entered into discussion about philosophy and scientific developments.

For Lidgett, the doctrine of the atonement was a key issue. Relationship with God is primary – much more important, in fact, than opinions about biblical inspiration or authority. Moreover, relationship with God is the ground of involvement in social concerns. Therefore, the atonement which effects this relationship is Lidgett's main theme [59].

> 59. The Atonement is not an ordination of the bare will of God without intrinsic relation to the salvation which is effected by it. It is not a satisfaction to the personal rights or to the affronted majesty of God. The fundamental condition of fatherly satisfaction is that it shall satisfy the fatherly by perfecting the filial. By virtue of His fatherhood, the Father is the guardian of the law of righteousness, which protects the family bond of love and fellowship. And this principle, as we have seen, has its supreme exemplification in God's dealings with mankind in the cross.
>
> *Source*: John Scott Lidgett, *The Spiritual Principle of the Atonement*, Epworth Press 1897, p. 301.

Lidgett says flatly, 'No distinctive contribution to the doctrine of the Atonement has been made by Methodist writers.'[8] He mentions only the work of Wesley and Watson and, interestingly, says that W. B. Pope, whom he much admires, helped reinforce the doctrine of God's Fatherhood, but did not discern its implications for atonement theology. Lidgett, however, hopes to make a contribution and, to understand it, we must see how he interprets the previous history of the doctrine, especially since the middle of the nineteenth century.

This particular history begins with J. McLeod Campbell's book, *The Nature of the Atonement* (2nd edn 1867). Until this time, the principal interest in the doctrine of the atonement had been the relation of Jesus' death to God; with Campbell there is a change of emphasis to the human dimension of the atonement.

Campbell, starting from the fatherhood God and the graciousness which that implies, assumes that the incarnation reflects perfect sonship in relation to God, a perfect relationship into which human beings cannot, of themselves, enter. Jesus, as incarnate, so identifies with human life that he recognizes the radical separation of human beings from God. Moreover, in response to that situation, Jesus is perfectly contrite, perfectly repenting for the alienation and perfectly acknowledging, with a deep 'Amen', the justice of the separation. Atonement occurs when human beings identify with Jesus in renewed relationship with God [60].

> 60. The liberty to call God Father, which we feel in the light of the revelation of the Father to us by the Son, we in that light *cannot but feel*; for in that light we not only apprehend the divine fatherliness, through perfect response of sonship yielded to it by the Son of God in humanity, and, at the same time, the sonship itself, which is that response, but we have this apprehension necessarily in personal reference to ourselves.
>
> *Source*: John McLeod Campbell, *The Nature of the Atonement*, 2nd edn 1867, pp. 300–301.

Campbell writes: 'Assuming the Incarnation, I have sought to realize the divine mind in Christ as perfect sonship towards God and perfect brotherhood towards men; and doing so the Incarnation has appeared, developing itself naturally and necessarily as the Atonement.'[9] The root of atonement is not the anger but the love of God; atonement expresses the graciousness which is the very nature of God.

Frederick Denison Maurice – according to Lidgett himself, the most important influence on his own thought – continued the exploration of the human dimensions of the atonement.[10] For Maurice, Jesus came to identify with the human, fallen condition; but in that condition he fulfilled, as he alone was able to do, the intended will of God. Self-surrender is the vital principle. The obedience of Jesus found its final and crowning triumph in the cross. But, Lidgett points out, no experience of death as a punishment for sin is involved, nor is the death of Christ set forth as meeting the demand of God, as the prerequisite of forgiveness. The death of Christ declares that the chasm between God and human beings is overcome but does not meet any demands which otherwise stand in the way of forgiveness. The atonement, therefore, expresses mercy but is not itself a cause of that mercy.

Again, B. F. Westcott's, *The Victory of the Cross* (1888) emphasizes Jesus' identification with the human condition. In contrast to our stunted moral perceptions, 'Christ in perfect sinlessness gave the power of a perfect estimate of sin,' and 'in this sense Christ suffered, knowing the nature of sin, knowing the judgment of God, realizing in every pain the healing power of a Father's wisdom. And in this sense the virtue of His Passion remains in its eternal power.'[11] Christ by his response, awakens our sympathy and imitation. But, Lidgett objects, Westcott does not indicate clearly what Jesus' death means.

Lidgett then mentions Horace Bushnell and Albrecht Ritschl as two theologians who had strenuously opposed any doctrine of satisfaction on account of sin. Bushnell maintains that 'Love itself is an essentially vicarious principle.'[12] The sacrifice of Christ is a manifestation in time of the eternal travail of God; it is the supreme example of true love expressing itself as suffering-redemption. Ritschl in his *Justification and Reconciliation* (1872) – Lidgett renders the title *Justification and Atonement* – also concentrates upon the human Jesus, the historical power of the incarnation and Jesus' self-consciousness as the source of all knowledge of God. Understanding of God is found only in Jesus, in the ethical community founded by Jesus and in a living relationship with him.

Jesus Christ, for Ritschl, is known in terms of what he is to us; we cannot draw metaphysical implications or know the truth of propositions about the pre-existence of transcendent entities. The revelation of God is made to us, in and through the relation in which God stands to his Son, and to the ethical community, the church, founded by his Son.[13] The idea of God as love demands as its correlate the kingdom of God, the ethical community in which the love of God is manifest. The atonement is therefore a subjective change in the hearts of individuals, and thus the realization of the ethical community which is the correlate and object of God's love. Ritschl's rejection of any satisfaction required by God is a direct reflection of his own philosophical position. Lidgett claims, however, that it is also an elimination of one of the most important aspects of the atonement.

The climax of earlier discussion is R. W. Dale's, *The Atonement* (1875). In this book Dale keeps the human dimension, but he emphasizes, as the others have not, that Jesus' death is the satisfaction for sin by being the endurance of penal suffering. Dale, instead of making this claim on the grounds of God's nature, speaks of God being subject to a natural law that is independent of him, although alive in him. Thus, because Dale does not believe that the atonement can be a presentation to God by God's own self, it can only be a presentation, i.e., satisfaction, made to the eternal law of righteousness. Lidgett, however, rejects the idea of an eternal law external to God and attempts to root the tension within God's own self [61].

---

61. It must be borne in mind that the Father stands for the Godhead in demanding the sacrifice; the Son stands for the Godhead in presenting it. The unity and eternal co-operation of the Persons of the Holy Trinity involve that all are with the Father in His demand, and that all are with the Son in His satisfaction; while the special relations of the divine Persons to one another and to man involve that the demand is made by the Father and satisfied by the Son. The unity of the Godhead in the Atonement must be carefully maintained.

Source: John Scott Lidgett, *The Spiritual Principle of the Atonement*, Epworth Press 1897, p. 282.

Lidgett, having conducted this survey in humility and with appreciation of the suggestions of each of these writers, now claims that the picture is too complex to yield a simple statement of what has been learned. Nonetheless, he insists that any statement of the nature and grounds of the atonement must meet the spiritual sensitivity and intellectual probing of these positions.[14]

The contribution which Lidgett hopes to make is to reclaim the significance of the notion of satisfaction so that the atonement is seen in its totality as something done by God, for God and for human beings [62]. Three points, he says, are consistently found in scripture: the atonement 'has Godward significance; it consists in our Lord's endurance of death on our behalf; and the spirit in which He underwent death – his great obedience – is of vital importance to the efficacy of His sacrifice'.[15]

---

62. When the Son who is given becomes Incarnate, it is apparent from all that has been previously said, that the bearing of sin on our behalf is necessary to Him. God is wroth with a race that misses the mark for which He created it; yet only His gift of His son can bring about its fulfilment of the ends of its creation, and this only through the atoning death which both gives full expression to the loving purpose and mercy of God, and turns away the wrath that is the manifestation of love against the sin which defeats its gracious ends. Thus the greatness of the demand is the measure of grace.

Source: John Scott Lidgett, *The Spiritual Principle of the Atonement*, Epworth Press 1897, pp. 306–7).

We have spent time with Lidgett's interpretation of the atonement because it is the most distinctive contribution to this topic among Methodists. Lidgett attempts to understand the character of God as grace expressed in creation, as wrath over human failure, and as reclaiming love directed on the cross both to God and to human beings. It is difficult to keep all of these aspects together, as the history of interpretations makes clear. But Lidgett, who reviews this history with great insight, carefully attempts to keep a proper weighting of the many factors in the atonement.

Then, in true Wesleyan spirit, he draws the practical implications of his interpretation, namely, the recreation of human life in both personal and corporate terms. He focusses the issue in these words: 'From all of these considerations it follows that the renewal and perfecting of society is the task set before those whose life is rooted in Christ and inspired by the Christian hope. Of that renewal and

perfecting the resurrection of our Lord is the pledge, the Holy Spirit is the power, the holy city is the pattern. It consists, however, in the prevalence of the spirit of the cross, and is brought about by the method of the cross.'[16]

Lidgett's book was widely used in Methodist theological colleges. Most of his Methodist successors, however, do not seem to make use of his work but move back to the human-ward dimensions of the atonement, especially under the guidance of psychology. Nevertheless Lidgett's contribution stands as a serious and sustained effort to see the atonement in all its aspects.

Other theologians

Several other Methodist theologians pursued the issue of the atonement, among them William F. Lofthouse (1871–1965), who in 1906 wrote *Ethics and Atonement* and in 1921, *Altar, Cross and Community*. Lofthouse raises ethical questions about traditional views of the atonement. The inherited views of God's sovereignty, omnipotence and honour and of the requirement of his satisfaction involved, in his view, a violation of human ethical integrity. Though ethical qualities can be encouraged by biblical passages, especially those which dwell on the character of Jesus, nonetheless, morality appears to be prior to religious or theological understanding. The reconciliation of God and human beings, therefore, must be understood in a way which is true to the nature of moral relationships among people. God, after all, seeks human beings themselves, not something other than them.

Lofthouse's thesis is that Jesus entered our situation, was present with us, suffered with us and therefore brings us to God by arousing our contrition. This is, in effect, a repetition of MacLeod Campbell's interpretation of Jesus as perfectly contrite. Lofthouse emphasizes the potency of Jesus' thorough identification with us to prompt our identification with him and thus to overcome our separation from God. In this way, he goes beyond the substitutionary interpretation of the atonement in a way which emphasized the integrity of God and of human beings. Indeed, one might say that, for Lofthouse, the incarnation says a great deal about human beings as well as about Divine Being.

In 1924 Maldwyn Hughes in his study, *What is the Atonement? A Study of the Passion of God in Christ*, continues Lofthouse's argument and, at the same time, attempts to be more inclusive. Indeed, his contribution is not so much that he proposed new answers as that, by retaining some of the concepts from other arguments, he kept the issue alive.

The work of W. Russell Maltby (1866–1951) in *Christ and His Cross* (1935) was also important. His position was based upon confidence that the life and teaching and, indeed, the consciousness of Jesus could be known and, when known, could reveal God's coming to us in him [63].

---

63. The cross of Christ assures us that we live our lives in the presence of a love which the worst of human sin could not quench and death itself could not destroy. Because God is love, He did not wait to be sought, but came forth, in Jesus Christ, to seek and to save that which was lost, and still His pursuit goes on until He finds us one by one. He did not need to be reconciled to us, but took up the task of reconciling our selfish hearts to Himself.

Source: W. R. Maltby, 'The Meaning of the Cross', London n.d., *c.* 1926, p. 17.

The attractive power of Jesus is a central theme [64]. God has come to us that we may come to God. The title of Maltby's Cato lecture, *Christ and His Cross*, states succinctly what he himself wanted to say: the cross is deeply imbedded in the life of Christ, and the life of Christ is focally expressed in the cross. The two are so interrelated that neither can be separated from the other. He writes: 'If we . . . regard his ministry as one continuous whole, and hold to the clues which his own words and deeds supply, we see all the meanings of his life converge and deepen, grow in majesty and scope until they are consummated in His death.'[17]

---

64. The question will be raised whether such a view of the meaning of the death of Christ is adequate to the Christian declaration that Christ bore our sins. If by such an expression we mean that our guilt was in some way transferred to Him, or that in His death He offered to God some kind of moral equivalent which made it possible for God to conceal and forgive our sins, the argument of these pages offers no contribution to such a theory. But if to bear sins means to go where the sinner is, and refuse either to leave him or to compromise with him; to love a shameful being, and therefore to be pierced by his shame; to devote oneself utterly to his recovery; and follow him with ceaseless ministries, knowing that he cannot be recovered without his consent, and that his consent may be indefinitely withheld – if this is to bear sin, then this is what Jesus did upon the cross, and it is the innermost secret of the heart of God.

Source: W. R. Maltby, 'The Meaning of the Cross', London n.d., *c.* 1926, p. 14.

C. Ryder Smith, in his *The Bible Doctrine of Salvation: A Study of the Atonement* (1941), exemplifies a dominant interpretation in the first half of the twentieth century. He argues that every doctrine of the atonement reflects the general knowledge or ethos of its time and that, in the twentieth century, psychology is the dominant thought form. 'Everyone is a psychologist – or thinks he is – modern theories of the Atonement therefore, in one way or another, use psychological analogies.'[18]

Smith acknowledges, at the same time, that psychological thought-forms are inadequate to reveal the full meaning of God's saving action but holds, nevertheless, that what we can understand with their help is worth knowing. Finding psychology to be particularly useful because it helps us to understand both individuals and groups, Smith puts special emphasis on the social or organic dimension of human existence.

Psychology offers four dimensions for understanding the atonement. First, if one is to do anything to save another, in the sense of changing character, one must identify with them. Next, one must know what it is like to be the other person without being like them. Third, one must feel the horror of the other's sin more than the other feels it. Fourth, the other must consent to be 'at one' with the person who saves him.

Smith insists that this is a description and not an explanation. Nonetheless, such description may help us to appreciate the significance of the atonement. Smith's position is built upon the fundamental reality of a 'fellowship' which is established between God and human beings. He offers what he calls a 'societary theory','which claims that 'Christ by his Incarnation, Death, Resurrection, does everything for us in the realm of Salvation, and through his indwelling spirit, does everything good in us'.[19] 'To speak after the manner of men, it does "make a difference" to God that He is now in fellowship with His child. The fact that there is fellowship is itself a difference on both sides.'[20] 'The societary doctrine, being in terms of fellowship, knows nothing of a God who waits in anger, or even waits aloof, for someone else to do something. He "sends the Son", and then welcomes the sinner.'[21]

Vincent Taylor explores the atonement in several volumes and both his account of the New Testament material and his theological interpretation are comprehensive and rich in insight. A principal work, *The Atonement in New Testament Teaching* (1940), summarizes his position [65] by saying that the atonement is the work of God which creates a relationship of true and abiding fellowship, not only with humankind but with the entire cosmos. Further, the atonement implies that persons are reconciled not only to God but to one another.[22]

> **65**. This truth of the underlying purpose of God to redeem men and reconcile them to Himself is the foundational principle of the doctrine of the Atonement, the touchstone by which erroneous theories are revealed, the heart of the preacher's message, and the religious basis for Christian worship and devotion.
>
> *Source*: Vincent Taylor, *The Atonement in New Testament Teaching*, Epworth Press 1940, p. 172.

The work of Christ is seen as being vicarious, representative and sacrificial. Each of these words is used in different ways in the New Testament. Since there is no single, consistent meaning, these notions must be combined in creative and constructive ways; and this is the task of the theologian who uses the biblical material as a primary resource. Taylor is opposed to substitutionary theories as not in keeping with New Testament usage, for sacrifice cannot be explained in legal categories. The work of Christ is vicarious because it is representative and representative because it is sacrificial. All of these concepts are combined under the theme of God's grace, which is at work to win sinners to a new relationship [66]. 'What is required is a category of representative action which, far from suggesting a purely external work of Christ passively accepted, includes within itself the transcendent deed of Christ on which redemption rests, and, at the same time, a human response so intimately related to it that, with no claim to personal merit, man can find true reconciliation with God.'[23] Finally, he emphasizes that, if this is the case, it is especially important to give to the eucharist a prominent place in our worship.

> **66**. It is not alone by his death that Christ brings us to God; it is also by his life, resurrection, and present mediatorial ministry on high. Calvary is the focal point of the ministry in terms of history; it is the place where we see God in the plenitude of His reconciling love . . . The Incarnation, culminating in death, is the expression in time of the Eternal Sacrifice within the heart of God.
>
> *Source*: Vincent Taylor, *The Atonement in New Testament Teaching*, Epworth Press 1940, p. 214.

In reviewing these developments in the interpretation of the atonement, we find that there is an effort to enlarge understanding beyond the narrow boundaries of satisfaction. There is also an attempt to keep the sense of the costliness of salvation through the coming of God in Jesus Christ. It is the historical Jesus who has the greatest importance for human beings in that, through their relationship to him, they are able to relate to God.

The atonement achieves the at-one-ment of the

Divine and the human, of the human and the Divine, and the use of such terms as 'spiritual', 'ethical', 'contrition', and 'fellowship' indicates the new directions in interpretation, stressing the full participation of God and human beings.

After the intense discussion of the atonement during the first decades of this century, there ensued a pause when the doctrine moved from the centre of theological attention. In recent years, however, there has been a fresh investigation of this theme. In 1991 the *Epworth Review* initiated a twelve-part series of articles on the atonement. Two of the articles by Methodists are especially thoughtful and shed light on current efforts to interpret this doctrine.

David Pailin, Professor of the Philosophy of Religion in the University of Manchester, probes questions about the understanding of God in traditional theories, namely, that God is hostile towards human beings because of their sin and therefore must be appeased (vol. 18, no. 3). The problem, Pailin argues, is not that God is offended by what people do, even though classical efforts to interpret atonement have often started with this presupposition. The real source of estrangement between God and human beings is not that persons are distant from God because of their creaturehood or because of their wilful and intentional sin; rather, human beings are estranged by their stupid and stubborn refusal to recognize what is truly good. In the life and death of Jesus Christ the loving character of God is presented and human beings are invited to acknowledge that which is good, namely, gracious acceptance by God and the life with him which results from it.

Frances M. Young, Edward Cadbury Professor of Theology at the University of Birmingham, wrote the first article in the series (vol. 18, no. 2). Professor Young particularly stresses – see also her *Sacrifice and the Death of Christ* (1975) – the relation of sin and suffering and of creation to atonement as well as the responsibility of God for the 'gone-wrongness' of the world.

In her *Can These Dry Bones Live?* (2nd edn 1992) Young more thoroughly explores possible contemporary meanings of this doctrine. She assesses the three major types of atonement theory as delineated by Gustav Aulen in *Christus Victor*: namely, the theories of Anselm and Abelard, and the theory, indicated by Aulen's title, which he finds both in the New Testament and Martin Luther. Then, having indicated the strengths and weaknesses of each interpretation, she presents a different, and in her view more satisfying, theory.

Her fresh statement uses two key resources: the apocalyptic setting of the doctrine and an enriched understanding of sacrifice. The apocalyptic theme emphasizes God's incarnate coming into the world at a time of crisis, when good and evil are in mortal struggle. The atonement is the establishment of God's presence in the midst of this battle [67].

Her discussion places the theme of sacrifice within the largest possible Old and New Testament setting, with emphasis upon sin and guilt but also upon worship and praise, and upon the unity of God with human beings and of persons with God.

---

67. Atonement . . . is the integration of the deep tensions built into God's world. Atonement is necessary because the very act of creation implies allowing the creation autonomy, it implies God abandoning his creation to be itself. Atonement is effected by God's presence in the midst of everything which denies him, everything which proclaims his absence. Now sacrifice, if it be the restoration of fellowship, the re-uniting of God with his creatures, if it be true worship, the declaration of God's praises and submission to his will, then it is at the very heart of the atoning process. The sacrifice of Christ was not a bribe to buy off God's anger, nor was it simply an expression of God's love for us. It was the mutual participation of God and man in a costly effort to reintegrate what had been torn asunder.

Source: Frances Young, *Can These Dry Bones Live?*, SCM Press, 2nd edn 1992, p. 78.

The emphases upon both the broken condition of the created order and the necessity to live within it with hope of renewal through sacrifice make this interpretation distinctive. The gospel of Jesus Christ provides the power to live with hope, even in the tension created by sin and evil. In Jesus Christ God has taken the initiative to be present with the creation which has become alienated from him. Indeed, one can say that God as creator, assuming responsibility for the malformation which has occurred in the creation, is present to overcome the destructive forces of evil, and that this presence is the expression of atonement and the ground of hope.

For both Pailin and Young, in very different ways, the doctrine of the atonement continues to be a central theme in Methodist theological exploration.[24]

Conclusion

In this chapter we have reviewed three of the most characteristic interests of twentieth-century Methodist theology: biblical study, the theology of experience and the doctrine of the atonement. Much constructive work has been done, and we can appreciate the faithfulness of these theologians, in intention and achievement, as they presented the gospel to their era. At the same time, we must recognize that this was a time of transition, of movement into new areas, of preparation for new and different times.

For discussion

1. In what ways, if at all, did the great twentieth-century Methodist biblical scholars influence the biblical understanding of ordinary Methodists?

2. Methodist biblical scholars, the chapter tells us, have shown the relationship of the biblical text both to an original historical context and to a continuing interpretive tradition. Are you conscious of a distinctively Methodist way of interpreting the Bible?

3. Consider what the chapter says about the senses in which 'experience' has been used in theology. What does the phrase 'Christian experience' mean to you? Is your understanding of Christian experience 'extended' by your understanding of the atonement?

4. Do the interpretations of the atonement by leading Methodist theologians help you to understand the meaning of the Cross? If so, how? If not, why?

5. For Lidgett, there is a direct link between his understanding of the cross and a Christian commitment to the recreation of human life in both personal and corporate terms. Is there the same link in your mind? Is it dependent upon a particular theory of the atonement?

6

Holiness, Church, Practical Theology

In the twentieth century, certain characteristic theological themes reflect what may be described as the sinews of the Methodist tradition. In this chapter we continue our survey and concentrate on Christian holiness, the doctrine of the church and the style and content of practical theology. In each case we will attempt a short review of the development of these emphases and consider those thinkers who have made relevant contributions.

Christian holiness

The doctrine of Christian holiness has retained a special place in Methodist theological sensibilities. Not always well understood or vigorously interpreted, it has nevertheless remained a strong element in Methodist self-understanding [68]. The power of God not only to forgive sin but also to create new beings in Jesus Christ, to make faith effective through

> **68.** The difference between receiving the Spirit, and being filled with the Spirit, is a difference not of kind, but of degree. In the one case, the light of heaven has reached the dark chamber, disturbing night, but leaving some obscurity and some deep shadows. In the other, that light has filled the whole chamber, and made every corner bright.
>
> *Source*: William Arthur, *The Tongue of Fire*, London 1856, p. 32.

love and to encourage Christian maturity have continued as dynamic impulses in Methodist theology.

John Wesley

Wesley regarded the doctrine of scriptural holiness or Christian perfection as 'the grand depositum which God has lodged with the people called Methodist' and he judged that 'for the sake of propagating this chiefly He has appeared to have raised us up'.[1] Over the years, however, commitment to the exploration, interpretation and affirmation of holiness within Methodism has varied in strength. Adam Clarke, for example, treated holiness as important in experience and doctrine, whereas Richard Watson paid meagre attention to it in his theological work. In general, concern for holiness has influenced Methodist practice more than Methodist theological investigation.

William Arthur

In the mid-nineteenth century William Arthur (1819–1901) revived interest in this doctrine. His book, *The Tongue of Fire* (London 1856), was a popular and powerful tract for the times. By means of a compelling, almost breathless, narrative of the history of the Holy Spirit in initiating and empowering Christian life, it presented a vibrant witness to the Spirit's continuing presence. Arthur was an orator, and here was an orator's evocation of the centrality of the Holy Spirit in Christian existence [69]. Continuing to be reprinted for a century, the book was widely influential in ecumenical circles, especially among holiness advocates. It concentrates more, however, on the power and presence of the Spirit than on specific aspects of his work.

---

69. The operation of the Holy Spirit implies a quickening of the nature of man by an impartation of the Divine nature, and every increase of it implies a fuller communion of the Eternal Father with His adopted child. When the soul of man is 'filled with the Holy Ghost', then has God that wherein He does rejoice, 'a temple, not made with hands' . . . In that living temple He can manifest truth, purity, tenderness, forgiveness, justice – the whole round of such attributes as His children below the sky are capable of comprehending.

Source: William Arthur, *The Tongue of Fire*, London 1856, pp. 38–39.

Holiness, as a work of the Holy Spirit, could be interpreted in terms of either personal or social change. Mainstream Methodist understanding tended to concentrate on the transformation of individuals, but there was a recurring disquietude if its expression in social concerns was played down or ignored [70].

William Burt Pope

Pope continued the tradition of taking the issue of holiness seriously and in his *Compendium* volume III discussed the doctrine carefully. Pope understood holiness to be a matter of maturation which affected the total character of a person, especially in the development of Christian qualities or virtues. He particularly stressed the work of the Holy Spirit in accomplishing transformation. At the same time, he was uncomfortable with the notion of 'perfection' because it seemed to imply an absolutism which he did

not find to be true to Christian existence. Indeed, he goes counter to Wesley in his insistence that to claim

---

70. It is no surprise to those who have inherited the teaching of Perfect Love to find that Wesley and his followers were noted for their activity in all manner of social work and help. In fact, most of the benevolent and religious agencies which characterize modern Christianity can be traced back to the Evangelical movement. Here were found the principles which made the slave trade impossible. Very early the needs of poorer members of the society were helped by gifts of clothes, money, and employment, and by sick visitation. For the relief of the outside poor there was . . . a Strangers' Friend Society . . . dispensary help . . . an orphanage . . . popular literature. It was impossible to seek to love God with all the heart without going on to love the neighbour as oneself.

Source: William T. A. Barber, 'The Rise and Progress of Methodism' in J. Scott Lidgett and Bryan H. Reed (eds), *Methodism in the Modern World*, Epworth Press 1929, pp. 18–19.

---

perfection is contrary to being holy. Viewing sanctification as both 'progressive and perfect', he believes that grace completely forgives and underwrites new growth. Holiness proceeds by degrees but reaches toward completeness.

Pope was also uneasy with the idea of 'second blessing' or a 'second work of grace' (understood as effecting, at an advanced spiritual stage, a conscious, decisive commitment like that experienced in the inaugurating moment of conversion) and with the notion of human contribution to perfection, both of which he found among some North American holiness leaders. Holiness, for Pope, had to do with quality of character, not with achievement of status; it was dynamic, maturing and always moving towards a goal which extended beyond its grasp [71].

A chief problem with discussions of holiness is a tendency either to be too specific about the holy life or to talk only in generalities. Consequently, holiness may be characterized in too rigid and static a fashion or too loosely and imprecisely.

71. . . . Sanctification is here viewed as a blessing bestowed freely under the covenant of grace . . . As a privilege of the covenant, its principle is twofold: purification from sin, consecration to God; holiness being the state resulting from these. As a gift of grace, it is declared to be perfect in the design of the Spirit; and full provision is made for the Entire Sanctification of the believer in the present life, even as full provision is made for his finished Righteousness and perfect Sonship.

Source: William Burt Pope, *A Compendium of Christian Theology*, III, 2nd edn, New York 1886, p. 28.

72. The most dangerous perversion of the Gospel, viewed as affecting individuals, is, when it is looked upon as a salvation for the soul after it leaves the body, but no salvation from sin while here. The most dangerous perversion of it, viewed as affecting the community, is, when it is looked upon as a means of forming a holy community in the world to come, but never in this. Nothing short of the general renewal of society ought to satisfy any soldier of Christ; and all who aim at that triumph should draw much inspiration from the King's own words: 'All power is given unto me in heaven and in earth.'

Source: William Arthur, *The Tongue of Fire*, London 1856, p. 87.

A 'second blessing'

Within British Methodism there was a group which wanted to specify the moral qualities of holiness and which interpreted holiness in the concrete terms of a 'second blessing'. In their publication *Joyful News*, and particularly through the influence of Thomas Champness's *Plain Talk on Perfection* (1897) and J. A. Beet's *Holiness as Understood by the Writers of the Bible: A Bible Study* (1880), the theological perspective of this movement was set out. Thomas Cook, who in 1902 produced *New Testament Holiness*, also contributed to the statement of this position. It should be noted, however, that both those for and those against the notion of 'second blessing' agreed that, fundamentally, holiness is God's gift of grace. It is not a human achievement. It is rather evidence of God's saving activity, remaking human life, both individual and corporate [72].

New Testament piety

In 1951 A. Raymond George published *Communion with God in the New Testament*, which was a sustained, meticulous investigation of prayer in the New Testament, revealing that communion which functions as 'the heart of the Christian faith' and extends into the whole of Christian life. New Testament piety, as George describes it, has such comprehensive power that '. . . nothing can refashion a man's *nature* so much as being in Christ. Thereafter,

as long as he remains in Christ, he will grow towards fuller sanctification, that is, will acquire a certain Christlikeness of character' (pp. 258–89). Using, then, this understanding of prayer as a key, George goes on to explore other dimensions of Christian experience, culminating in sanctification.

Christian perfection

The doctrine of Christian perfection is not peculiar to Methodists, and John Wesley rejected the notion that he had invented it. He affirmed, rather, that he found it in the promises of the Christian gospel and in the teaching of a long and impressive line of Christian thinkers. The lives of saints pointed to its experienced reality and theological reflection located it within the complex of grace, responsive love, and Christian maturity.

Methodists have produced some of the best histories of the doctrine. In addition to W. B. Pope's treatment in his *Compendium*, volume III, there is H. W. Perkins's *The Doctrine of Christian Perfection* (1927) and Frederick W. Platt's article on 'Perfection (Christian)' in the *Encyclopedia of Religion and Ethics*.[2]

Changing emphases

Yet there were significant changes in emphasis over the years. Henry D. Rack writes: 'It might be too much to claim that Methodist Theology by the end of the nineteenth century had deepened and widened Wesley's idea of holiness; but at least some men had begun to see that religion could not be merely individualistic; could not be a private concern unrelated to society except by way of individual charity. Hughes' sermons mark a definite change of emphasis in this respect; and it is significant that he criticized the Anglican Evangelical "holiness" convention of the 1880s because they lacked an ethical and social application'.[3]

The most significant study, however, is *The Idea of Perfection in Christian Theology* (1934) by R. Newton Flew (1886–1962). In this historical study, Flew surveys Christian teaching from the New Testament to Albrecht Ritschl and confirms the place of 'perfection' at the heart of the Christian tradition. He concludes that the doctrine of perfection must not be understood as a static achievement of the final goal of life with God but, rather, as a supernatural or eternal destiny, which in this life may be realized in singular love of God. In his view, significant growth in Christ is possible in human history, and this possibility constitutes the very character of true Christian existence. To love God perfectly stands before all Christians as the purpose of life and the meaning of salvation – a challenge to maturity and a gift of grace [73].

---

73. The doctrine of Christian perfection – understood not as an assertion that a final attainment of the goal of the Christian life is possible in this world, but as a declaration that a supernatural destiny, a relative attainment of the goal which does not exclude growth, is the will of God for us in this world and is attainable – lies not merely upon the by-paths of Christian theology, but upon the high road.

Source: R. N. Flew, *The Idea of Perfection in Christian Theology*, OUP 1934, p. 397.

Flew maintains, too, that the love of God is concretely manifest in daily work, in the regular vocation of people in the ordinary course of life. Saintliness is not living apart from the usual tasks of life or separating the secular from the sacred; rather, it is living in the regular tasks and offering daily work to God. Every task can become a service rendered to one's neighbours and therefore an offering of love and life to God. The offering of life with this completeness is the meaning of Christian perfection.

A Charles Wesley hymn captures Flew's central understanding and he quotes it in his conclusion.

> Yet when the work is done,
> The work is but begun:
> Partaker of Thy grace,
> I long to see Thy face;
> The first I prove below,
> The last I die to know.

No doctrine is stagnant, no teaching remains unchanged over time and through changing situations. In the case of Christian holiness, its character as both a hope and an achievable goal is kept, but theologians weigh the two aspects differently, and each generation attempts to revive what it believes predecessors have neglected. Flew's study, uncovering the long history of commitment to love of God and neighbour and the importance of saintly living, must be seen against this background. The fact that he undertook it and attempted to reinvigorate the doctrine is certainly due to his being a Methodist.

Later studies

The theme of Christian holiness was significantly continued in the work of W. E. Sangster (1900–1960). In 1943 he published *The Path to Perfection* which was both a doctoral dissertation and a call to renewed interest in holy living. His most thorough study is his book *The Pure in Heart: A Study in Christian Sanctity* (1954). He writes 'The cardinal features of sanctity are alike wherever we meet it and the major elements of method are alike as well. Similarity to Jesus binds all of the saints together. Purity in prayer, faith and love . . . these are the salient characteristics in all the methods by which they ascended the heights.'[4]

Sangster insists that the possibility of sanctification is universal, for God's grace is free to all and for all and in all [74].

74.	Think not the faith by which the just shall live Is a dead creed, a map correct of heaven, Far less a feeling, fond and fugitive, A thoughtless gift withdrawn as soon as given; It is an affirmation and an act That bids eternal truth be present fact. *Source*: Hartley Coleridge, quoted by Sangster, *The Pure in Heart*, Epworth Press 1954, p. 221.

There are, for Sangster, three characteristics of saintliness [75]: a blinding realization of the love of God, an overwhelming love in response, and love's widening to embrace the world.[5]

To characterize the life of holiness, Sangster utilizes the fruit of the Spirit which is described in Galatians 5.22f.: love, joy, peace, longsuffering, kindness, goodness, faithfulness, meekness, temperance.

75.	Some saints, it is true, set out to be saints. But others have no such ambition in mind; no such thought. Consumed with the longing to aid their suffering fellowmen, the idea of their own holiness never seems to have crossed their utterly engrossed minds . . . they were so self-forgetting in service that it could be said of each of them what was said of Samuel Barnett of Toynbee Hall, 'He forgot himself to the extent of forgetting that he had forgotten.' *Source*: W. E. Sangster, *The Pure in Heart*, Epworth Press 1954, p. 137.

In 1958 the conviction that sanctification is and should remain a central theme of Methodism was reinforced by Eric Baker who in *The Faith of a Methodist* treats this as the central distinguishing mark of the tradition. To illustrate the nodal position of this doctrine, Baker explores the ways in which it has shaped understanding of God, of Jesus Christ, of the Holy Spirit, of sin and salvation and of the church. Baker, on his own admission, does not attempt to bring originality to the interpretation, but his book is fresh and makes clear how, for a recent Methodist leader, this doctrine is of central theological importance.

The goal of holiness, the developed character of holy living, the self-critical awareness of personal growth, the combination of the love of God and the love of neighbour, and the joyful living in fellowship with God all characterize Methodist spiritual intention. The fact that, as our brief survey reveals, this vision of the Christian life has been preserved is a continuing challenge to keep it in clear focus. The past of the Methodist tradition has bequeathed both spiritual achievement and spiritual ambition to its present.

Church and ministry

For Christians everywhere the twentieth century has been a time of church union. Churches which share an understanding of the Christian faith or a pattern of organization or both have been coming together to embody their unity in Christ. Moves towards union have also characterized British Methodist life. From early in the century different denominations that shared either origins or mission began to discuss the possibility of joining together. The process was, for many participants, slower and more difficult to achieve than was originally hoped. But in 1932 the Methodist Church in Great Britain came into existence.

From that point interest broadened to consider whether traditions that were less closely affiliated might also come together, and a primary interest developed in whether the Methodist Church and the Church of England could unite.

The possibility of church union raises, of course, in a very pointed way the question, 'What is a church?', closely followed by, 'What is the Methodist Church in Great Britain?' and 'How does this church relate to other bodies of Christians?'

To understand how Methodists have explored these topics and with what results, it is necessary, first of all, to look back and see how Methodism understood itself in the past.

Wesley's understanding of 'church'

Because John Wesley took Christian history seriously, respected the integrity of the early church and honoured his own Anglican tradition, the issue of how Methodism could be an authentic expression of the Body of Christ was, for him, of vital importance.

He understood the church in terms of Fellowship and Mission. The church, in other words, is defined by its faithfulness to the tasks which have been given by God and, for Methodism, this involved the spreading of Christian holiness throughout the land and maintaining a close community to support growth in faith and life [76]. Here, once again, can be seen clearly the interplay of practice and theory, of Christian experience and Christian theology, which characterizes Wesley's thought.

---

76. If there was any distinctive note that Methodism contributed to the doctrine of the Church it was the emphasis that it laid on Christian fellowship. These lovers of their Lord joined in the intimate society of the class meeting found a strange new love for one another . . . In 1743 John Wesley published *An Earnest Appeal to Men of Reason and Religion*, and at the end was a poem . . .

> Happy the souls that first believed,
> To Jesus and each other cleaved,
> Joined by the action from above
> In mystic fellowship of love!

Source: A. W. Harrison, 'The Church' in J. Scott Lidgett and Bryan H. Reed (eds), *Methodism in the Modern World*, Epworth Press 1929, p. 153.

How Methodism was regarded

The question of whether Methodism should be understood as an independent church or simply as a movement within the established church was not, initially, of great urgency. By mid-nineteenth century, however, the Tractarian movement within the Church of England questioned whether such bodies as Methodists could be regarded as churches.

At first, most Methodists were not greatly concerned. They were simply too busy, too engaged in their life and mission to be anxious. Some, however, were perturbed that fellow-Christians did not recognize their authenticity or legitimacy. Convinced, however, that they were operating under the guidance of the Holy Spirit and were obedient to the mission given by God, they moved ahead, allowing their own church life to develop and attempting to fit the form of their polity to the mission of their life. Methodists were consequently slow to spell out their understanding of the church or to use it to justify their existence.

The shaping of Methodist church life

The theme of the Holy Spirit's guidance in the shaping of Methodism, however, was persistently articulated. William Arthur in *The Tongue of Fire* (1856) had specially emphasized it, though his exposition focusses more on a spiritually endowed ministry than on common life in the Spirit. Benjamin Gregory's Fernley Lecture of 1873 [77], however, provides both a good statement of the Methodist tradition and a base on which ongoing interpretations would be founded.

---

77. The Church is the organ of the Spirit, and that in its individual members . . . The Church is a living organism, called into existence, created, shaped, animated, ensouled, actuated, by the Spirit.

Source: Benjamin Gregory, *The Holy Catholic Church, The Communion of Saints*, London 1873, p. 28.

William Strawson has succinctly summarized Gregory's position. 'Like the early Church, Methodism is first concerned with the preaching of the Gospel, and with the life of service to God and man which follows from its reception. Organization is a secondary matter and must serve the best interests of the Gospel; the Church is not called into being to set up an organization, but to witness. This implies that no organization can be regarded as essential or normative, and any attempt to define the Church so that others can be unchurched is repugnant to Methodists.'[6]

Growth and schism

The ecclesiastical reality of Methodism in Great Britain during the nineteenth century was that it experienced both remarkable growth and severe schism. The separations were over issues of church government – especially issues of democracy and lay leadership – not over matters of doctrine or basic understanding of mission. Nevertheless, when the effort to unite was made, resolution of polity issues was more quickly achieved than doctrinal agreement. Efforts at reunion began as early as 1902 and culminated in 1932 with the establishing of the new church. In 1926 a theological statement was approved – leadership was given especially by A. S. Peake and J. S. Lidgett but also by many others – and a doctrinal base for the Methodist Church was formulated. It is valuable to read this statement in full [78].

The statement itself is broad enough, or unspecific enough, to allow much variation of interpretation. There is, for instance, no reference to specific historic creeds or exactly which Protestant emphases had priority. But the ongoing need for interpretation of these relationships as the new church continues to define itself is clearly recognized.

The issues of the doctrine of the church, ministry and sacraments are all connected. There was general agreement that the structures of all churches are human constructs and do not reflect a definite form framed in the mind of Christ or proved in experience to be necessary. Openness of interpretation of the two sacraments – Baptism and the Lord's Supper – was accepted, but there was a problem about their administration, especially in the case of the Lord's Supper. For Wesleyan Methodists, this was the responsibility of the ordained ministers. For some of the other groups, the issue was bound up with the status of the local preacher and the practice of allowing lay participation in the distribution of the elements. There was therefore keen debate about the exact nature of ordination and the relation of the

78. The Methodist Church claims and cherishes its place in the Holy Catholic Church, which is the Body of Christ. It rejoices in the inheritance of the apostolic faith, and loyally accepts the fundamental principles of the historic Creeds and of the Protestant Reformation. It ever remembers that in the providence of God Methodism was raised up to spread Scriptural holiness through the land by the proclamation of the evangelical faith, and declares its unfaltering resolve to be true to its divinely appointed mission.

The doctrines of the evangelical faith, which Methodism has held from the beginning and still holds, are based upon the divine revelation recorded in the Holy Scriptures. The Methodist Church acknowledges this revelation as the supreme rule of faith and practice. These evangelical doctrines, to which the preachers of the Methodist Church, both Ministers and Laymen, are pledged, are contained in Wesley's *Notes on the New Testament* and the first four volumes of his *Sermons*.

The Notes on the New Testament and the Forty-four Sermons are not intended to impose a system of formal or speculative theology on Methodist preachers, but to set up standards of preaching and belief which should secure loyalty to the fundamental truths of the gospel of redemption, and ensure the continual witness of the Church to the realities of the Christian experience of salvation.

Source: The Deed of Union (1932), reprinted annually in *The Constitutional Practice and Discipline of the Methodist Church, Book 2*, Methodist Publishing House.

ordained ministry to the general ministry of all Christians. A compromise was reached [79] which allowed for variation of interpretation but which achieved a union and not simply a federation.

Interpretation of doctrine

Throughout the discussion of union, doctrine was important but, as we have seen, exact definition and a single authoritative interpretation were not sought. Indeed, the documents reveal a residual distrust of systematic construction and closed options. Doctrine

---

79. Christ's ministers in the Church are stewards of the household of God and shepherds of His flock. Some are called and ordained to the sole occupation, and have a principal and directing part in these great duties; but they hold no priesthood differing in kind from that which is common to all the Lord's people, and they have no exclusive title to the preaching of the Gospel or the care of souls. These are ministries shared with them by others, to whom also the Spirit divides his gifts severally as He wills.

Source: The Deed of Union (1932), reprinted annually in *The Constitutional Practice and Discipline of the Methodist Church, Book 2*, Methodist Publishing House.

---

is treated as a necessary foundation for union, but a foundation which must be elastic enough to encompass a wide variety of meanings. A strong pragmatic element is also evident: doctrine is seen as enabling practice rather than severely restricting it. For instance, the meaning of the Lord's Supper for those who participate was accepted as more important than who should administer it. Yet here, too, there was openness to differing interpretations. British Methodism was committed to Christian practice and only secondarily to the effort to devise tight doctrinal definition. 'Christian practice' was defined more by common ways of doing things than by reference to a controlling set of theological directions.

Methodist self-definition

But whatever the status of doctrine in general, there was need for a more adequate statement of the nature of the church itself. In the event, interest focussed on first understanding the Christian church in terms of its common rootage, its essential life and mission and its claims for community among all Christian people – and only then attempting to assess Methodism's place within that inclusive catholicity (see C. Ryder Smith, *The Sacramental Society*, 1927).

Prior to World War II, the person who contributed most to developing such a doctrine of the church was R. Newton Flew. Flew had shared in Methodism's self-definition as it moved towards the union of 1932. He was also a participant in ecumenical discussions, having attended in 1937 both the Oxford Conference on Life and Work and the Edinburgh Conference on Faith and Order. In both of these conferences there was extensive discussion of the idea of the *ecclesia* (the church). In that same year he served as convener of a committee that produced a report on 'The Nature of the Christian Church According to the Teaching of the Methodists'. This statement was adopted unanimously by the Methodist Conference of 1937.

The foundation of Flew's work was published in his important study, *Jesus and His Church* (1938). The main thesis of this book is that the church is not an accidental or even a happy addition to the ministry of Jesus, but rather an indispensable element in it. Jesus, in other words, intended to establish the church [80]; and the church is God's creation, not a voluntary assembly of people to serve a common purpose.

The church, moreover, is actually constituted by the work of the incarnate Word of God through the Holy Spirit and is concretely embodied in the preaching of the Word and the administration of the sacraments. Specifically, this means that the Word and the sacraments are not dependent upon an established office like the ordained ministry, but such an office is contingent upon the Word.

---

80. . . . three decisive moments may be discerned in the action of Jesus in constituting the Ecclesia. First, He 'called' the disciples and taught them. Second, he sent them forth to proclaim the good news that the new era had dawned, and their proclamation was both by word and in deed. Third, at the Last Supper He instituted the new covenant with them as representing the new people of God.

Source: R. Newton Flew, *Jesus and His Church*, Epworth Press 1938, p. 16.

Ecumenical vision

The delineation of these originating characteristics of the church led to an ecumenical vision of unity among several church bodies [81]. 'Today there is stirring in the minds of men a strong discontent with the present broken communion of the Ecclesia, and a fresh hope of a clearer expression in outward act and form, of its essential unity in Christ.'[7]

> 81. Since the gospel brings victory over sin and death, God has knit together the whole family of the Church in heaven and on earth in the communion of saints, united in the fellowship of service, of prayer and of praise; and the Church on earth looks forward to the vision of God, the perfect consummation of its present fellowship in the life of heaven.
>
> *Source*: *The Nature of the Christian Church According to the Teaching of the Methodists*. Affirmation 7, Methodist Publishing House, n.d., p. 40.

The work of Flew grounded the church in the intention of Jesus, made understanding the church prior to understanding church order, ministry or sacraments, and kept central an ecumenical vision. All of these points became important to ongoing Methodist interpretations of the church.

As Methodism reached the mid-twentieth century it affirmed the primacy of community for Christian existence, the guiding presence of the Holy Spirit and the inclusive embrace of all Christians in the body of Christ. Upon these foundations, Methodism engaged in vigorous effort to achieve increasing unity, first steps being taken to explore possibilities of union with the Church of England. Negatively, divisions among churches were viewed as disobedience to God's intention and an impediment to mission; positively, union among churches was viewed as enabling authentic and effective witness.

Practical theology

John Wesley, as we have presented him, understands theology as essentially a practical discipline; for him, that is to say, theory and practice cannot be separated and each affects the other. Consequently, theological understanding is for the purpose of guiding Christian existence, and Christian existence informs and shapes theological interpretation.

At the theological centre and holding everything together is the reality of God in Jesus Christ, who reveals the Father's intention in creation and redemption, and the Holy Spirit's work, effecting the transformation of individuals and of the cosmos. As we have seen, the main emphases of Wesley's theology are christologically centred, inclusively trinitarian and focussed on the transformation of all nature, including human nature; and these themes have provided the basic track along which the Methodist tradition has moved.

From understanding to practice

To assert that Methodist theology has been characterized by holding theological interpretation and active Christian practice together is not to claim that this tradition is unique. Other theologians and other traditions have had similar interests. Nor is it to maintain that representatives of the Methodist tradition have always kept the balance with the same intention or intensity. There is, in fact, a great variety of view among Methodist theologians. But it is to claim that a close inter-weaving of theological interpretation and practical application is characteristic of the Methodist tradition throughout [82].

> 82. Insofar as Methodism can claim to have a theology of the Spirit, its doctrine has been practical rather than speculative . . . These facts explain why Methodism, viewed historically, made practically no contribution to theology. It stressed certain aspects of truth . . . But its interest was always in life more than truth – or, rather, in truth which was creative of life. That is why what it had to say concerning the Holy Spirit narrows itself down to His work in conveying to the soul the forgiving grace of Christ and in producing the virtues of a holy nature and life.
>
> *Source*: A. E. Humphries, 'The Work of the Holy Spirit' in J. Scott Lidgett and Bryan H. Reed (eds), *Methodism in the Modern World*, Epworth Press 1929, p. 99.

Further, this claim is not made with the confidence that Methodist theologians have always been conscious of this method of theologizing. Instead, the approach has been expressed as an integral, permeative part of the Methodist pattern of Christian life and service. Methodist theology has been formulated by practitioners who have worked for and within the life of the church, preaching, serving circuits, leading mission projects, organizing social action movements, establishing hostels, working for church unity – and, withal, attempting to reflect about the Christian gospel in terms of its embodiment.

With heart and mind

To acknowledge that Methodism is not unique should not prevent us from recognizing its distinctive quality. Methodism has had to struggle, at all times, to keep a balance between the kind of activities just listed; and when it has failed, it has been more engaged in preaching and ordering the church's life than lost in thought. But it has attempted to serve God with mind as well as heart and strength fully involved.

A quick survey may help to make the point. Richard Watson, for instance, concentrated on the validity of scripture and the intellectual challenge of Deism, while leading Methodism's programme of mission and engaging widely in the official life of the denomination. Later in the nineteenth century, William Burt Pope concentrated on inherited doctrines from a rich diversity of sources, while affirming and exhibiting the singular importance of personal sanctity as the earnest expectation of all committed Christians [83].

William Arthur provides a third example. He was first of all a preacher and, as such, undertook to be a spokesman for the faith to his age. Intellectually, he confronted secularism and positivism; practically, he travelled the world proclaiming the faith. The two sides of his life were combined in his book on the Holy Spirit's work in individual human lives and general human history. In both Pope and Arthur we see the balance move from one side to the other, as each expresses and embodies their concern for both theory and practice.

83. Every doctrine has its ethical side: all truth returns in duty to Him who gave it . . . The Mediatorial Work of Christ is a congregation of revealed truths, each of which, whether referring to Himself or His work, has its moral bearing . . . The appropriation of personal salvation introduces a series of teachings which are as much ethical as dogmatic . . . It may be said that no doctrine is ever taught without reference to a corresponding human duty; nor is any duty taught for which a doctrinal reason is not given.

Source: William Burt Pope, *A Compendium of Christian Theology*, III, 2nd edn, New York 1886, p. 161.

Social responsibility

By the last decades of the nineteenth century, especially in Hugh Price Hughes, we find a restatement of evangelistic theology and the theme of gospel preaching tightly bound together with a radical emphasis on social action and responsibility. Hughes' writings were published sermons, and his sermons were calls to conversion and to the responsibilities of the converted. Here, in exemplary form, practical theology was expressed.

John Scott Lidgett is a special example of precisely this combination. He undertakes a strenuous investigation of the doctrines of the atonement and the Fatherhood of God, while establishing the Bermondsey Settlement and dealing knowledgeably and energetically with the practical problems of its neighbourhood [84].

The same interaction is found among scholars who were also preachers, class leaders and bearers of

84. From the outset of my career my main concern had been theological. So far from my educational and other social activities having been a departure from this concern, they have been entirely based upon my construction of what is involved in the Christian revelation of God and particularly in His Fatherhood.

Source: John Scott Lidgett, *My Guided Life*, Methuen 1936, p. 144.

responsibility in the life of the church. R. Newton Flew, for instance, when teaching at Wesley House, Cambridge and studying the relation of Jesus and the disciples to the establishment of the church, was at the same time engaged in promoting the union of those churches which had enough in common to become the Methodist Church in Great Britain, and looking beyond to possible larger unions.

To make such a selective survey may, of course, be a distortion either of the contribution of the individuals mentioned or of the tradition as a whole. Nevertheless, when one surveys this tradition and its major representatives, one is impressed by the remarkable manner in which thought serves action and action shapes thought. The modest claim being made, therefore, is that, from John Wesley down to the present, theology within Methodism has largely resisted becoming an independent, self-enclosed activity and that practical activity, though perhaps to a lesser degree, has been tied to ongoing attempts to understand the Christian gospel. For the most part, British Methodism has been neither non-intellectual nor anti-intellectual; rather, as it has sought to understand in order to change and has allowed change to underwrite fresh interpretation, it has been practically intellectual and intellectually practical.

Continuity

It is clear, from the last two chapters, that there has been important continuity of interest in the Methodist tradition. Fundamental tenets have remained important: the biblical base for theology, the primacy of experience, especially the experience of salvation through Jesus Christ's atoning work, the goal of Christian perfection, the significance of the church as the called community, and, through it all, the practical character of theological reflection. As a consequence,

Methodists have contributed to a theology of life and for life and to a vital witness of God's work in the world based on a complementarity of thought and action.

In retrospect, Methodists have probably been too modest in their assessment of their theological seriousness and their theological contribution. Accepting too readily the general notion that theology is an independent intellectual activity, they have echoed the judgment of persons who come from different doctrinal traditions that Methodist theology has not been significant. But the truth is otherwise: Methodism has embodied a tradition which has changed life and thought. It has contributed to understanding which has transformed life and life which has transformed understanding.

For discussion

1. How would you define 'Christian holiness'? Has Methodist teaching about holiness – in local practice, if not in the works of the theologians – been too individualistic?
2. Pope was 'uncomfortable with the notion of "perfection"', as indeed was John Wesley. Is the term so misleading today as to be a liability? Or is it an important expression of a characteristically Methodist 'optimism of grace'?
3. Examine the extracts on the church and the ministry in this chapter. How far do they express your own ideas? In what ways do you see things differently?
4. The emphasis on Christian fellowship was, according to A. W. Harrison, a distinctive note which Methodism contributed to the doctrine of the church. Is this a true and important claim or a piece of Methodist wishful thinking?
5. How do you understand 'practical theology'?

7

Contemporary Trends

Recent British Methodist theology has been permeated, or perhaps dominated, by ecumenical factors, and especially by the possibility of Methodism itself becoming part of a more inclusive church union. Theologically, this has had the result of concentrating attention on issues of two types: shared Christian beliefs and the complementarity of different traditions.

During the 1950s and 60s hard work was done, in preparation, it was hoped, for union with the Church of England. A Methodist majority supported the union but in two votes, in 1969 and 1972, the Church of England rejected the plan. Frustration was experienced not simply over the political failure but over what many believed was a rejection of the will of God for the churches. An opportunity was lost, but the thought and work involved was substantial and of continuing value. Indeed, such responsible and faithful endeavour provides the appopriate context for ongoing Methodist theological activity.

Theological diversity

In spite of this, however, there is theological diversity among Methodists. At one end of the spectrum, we find serious questioning of the viability of inherited theological formulations, while at the other there is a reaffirmation of the classical tradition. In between, attempts have been made to interpret Methodist beliefs in relation to both mainstream Christian doctrine and modern intellectual and moral issues. In Great Britain, therefore, present-day Methodist theo-

logy is characterized by ecumenical openness and by a concern to communicate Christian faith to the contemporary world.

British Methodist theology still recalls its Wesleyan heritage, but with caution. The Wesleys are appreciated, especially for John Wesley's social concern and organizational ability and for the invigorating contributions they both made to evangelism, hymnody and worship. Less attention is paid to their explicitly theological work, and there is resistance to the constraints of their theological frame of reference. John Wesley, in fact, is generally appreciated as the inaugurator of a movement rather than as a continuing theological guide.

There is even less theological interest in the intervening tradition of the nineteenth century and the first half of the twentieth. Little mention is made of such figures as Richard Watson, William Burt Pope, Hugh Price Hughes or John Scott Lidgett, and their work lies unused. Attention is fixed, rather, upon contemporary problems and prospects. The theological inquiries of these predecessors are taken to be so historically conditioned and their criticial and constructive work so encapsulated in their own time – in short, so significantly different – as to provide little guidance for present-day reflection or interpretation.

The tradition seems to have been chiefly effective through the continuing use of the Wesley hymns, the impact of preachers and the influence of teachers upon students in Methodist theological colleges [85]. Recognition of the Methodist tradition, therefore, is typically in the form of references to significant individuals, character formation and educational development. The tradition has lived more by participation in the life of the denomination than by definitive interpretation of outstanding theological contributions or of a deposit of theological texts. It has been passed along, as by osmosis, from one generation to another.

---

85. I am very sure that the greatest single asset we have in theological training is the tradition of our colleges, the thing which is bigger than the staff or the syllabus, because it embodies all the staffs and all the lectures and all the students who have ever lived within its walls – for if tradition does not exist in stones and building, it cannot long survive without them. That is why opening and closing a theological college is not to be disposed of at the economic level, as though one were discussing some utility project of public baths and wash-houses. Thomas Jackson and his companions helped to create a seminary tradition which has come to pervade all our colleges, and we have a responsibility not lightly and unadvisedly to mutilate the corporate life which they began.

Source: Gordon Rupp, *Thomas Jackson: Methodist Patriarch*, Epworth Press 1954, p. 32.

In a fundamental way, this mode of transmission is characteristic of Wesleyan and Methodist theology in that understanding is embedded in life, and practice is as significant as interpretation. At the same time, it makes following the continuities in the development of this tradition or specifying major contributions to its ongoing character extremely difficult.

Contemporary British Methodist theology lives in the present. It takes its actual situation with utter seriousness and intends to be a responsible mediator of the Christian gospel to its context. For this very reason, it looks less to the past and more to the future – a situation which, as William Strawson points out [86], can lead to a certain imbalance.

Questioning the legacy

At one end of the present Methodist theological spectrum may be placed the work of two former

---

86. It is to be admitted that, with one or two notable exceptions, Methodist theology is mainly of interest within the family of Methodism. Methodism has not in fact produced many outstanding scholars, and has depended upon other Churches for leadership in theological matters . . . There is no danger of Methodists going in for too theoretical a theology. But there is every reason to desire that there should be a continual interest, among preachers and people alike, in the great doctrines which have nurtured the Christian people throughout the centuries and still can nurture them.

Source: William Strawson, 'Methodist Theology 1870–1950' in Rupert Davies, A. Raymond George and Gordon Rupp (eds), *A History of the Methodist Church in Great Britain*, vol. 3, Epworth Press 1983, pp. 230–31.

Professors of Theology at the University of Bristol: John H. S. Kent and Kenneth Grayston. In his book *The End of the Line?*, John Kent takes the presuppositions of modern intellectual convictions (for him, Enlightenment sensibilities) so seriously that he questions the validity of inherited theology. He believes that theological efforts to restate rational orthodoxy or to develop liberal Protestantism have reached the end of their authenticity or usefulness.[1]

Committed to the aims of the Enlightenment, Kent argues that convincing contemporary theological statements must be made on the basis of faith-assumptions of three kinds: faith in the underlying rationality of the universe; faith in the quality of life commended by what seems to have been the teaching of Jesus; and faith in reason.

Kent completely rejects ecclesiastical claims to absolute truth or to the power to command the truth. Traditional rational dogmatics presumed the authority of privileged texts and ecclesiastical mandates; liberal Protestantism assumed that it could qualify, rather than replace, what Christians believe, having discovered the essence of faith beneath its traditional trappings. Both have failed, and contemporary people (Enlightenment people) are unwilling to accept either of these alternatives. For these people, with whom

Kent would align himself, traditional and recent formulations of Christian theological meaning no longer carry convincing power.

In other work, Kent had explored the Methodist tradition more thoroughly – for instance, in *The Age of Disunity* (1966). But in *The End of the Line?* his reading of Methodism's place within the history of Christian thought is focussed on a single topic. John Wesley's importance lies, he argues, in his teaching on Christian perfection, which attempted to preserve the possibility of holiness within a Christian community whose members lived and worked in the ordinary world. But 'In the history of the Christian Church Wesley's perfectionism was a brief episode.'[2] According to Kent, this was due in part to Wesley's confusion over the distinction between voluntary and involuntary transgression and in part to his stress on a specific event of experiencing perfection. Nevertheless, 'Wesley's doctrine of perfection represented an important attempt to revive the idea and pursuit of holiness (understood as a sinful condition, whatever the qualifications which Wesley sometimes applied), in a society which was now tempted to discard the idea of holiness altogether, and in which the Church, responding to the mood of the age, increasingly described the Christian life in limited moral terms.'[3]

But Wesley's contribution was within an ecclesiastical and intellectual context which could not and would not last, and the statement of doctrines assuming inherited convictions became increasingly untenable.

As a result, radical moves, more radical than liberal theologians have been willing to undertake, are now required [87]. Native human capacity for rational and moral action must be called upon. Anthropology must become the basis for theology.

Moral conviction, faithfulness to the spirit of Jesus Christ, is all that remains. But human beings are capable of making this response and this challenge might win the commitment of critical modern people. To present this possibility is, for Kent, the remaining task of theology.

Kenneth Grayston, an older colleague of Kent's at

---

87. And so a certain split has taken place. Certain kinds of religious behaviour belonged to and took place within the environment of the Churches; certain styles of religious thinking had for the moment ceased to belong to the environment of the Churches. J. S. Bezzant diagnosed this situation accurately some years ago:

I think it is entirely reasonable for any man who studies the spirit of the facing of life as Christ faced it, and his recorded teaching, to decide that by him he will stand through life, death or eternity rather than join in a possible triumph of evil over him. Whether or not any Church will regard such a man as a Christian is nowadays wholly secondary and manifestly relatively unimportant (*Objections to Christian Belief*, 1963, pp. 109–10).

Source: John H. S. Kent, *The End of the Line?*, SCM Press 1982, p. 131.

---

the University of Bristol, shares many of his convictions. In an article, 'Pilgrimage in Theology', *Epworth Review* (January 1978), he expresses discomfort with much inherited theology and calls for a clearer, simpler, more relevant statement of Christian beliefs. He states that he finds it possible to live with fewer theological affirmations than he once did. Much theology, he claims, has become too complicated and a number of notions simply superfluous, such as supernaturalism, interpretation of human life as fallen and of God as a concrete person. Such interpretations no longer have significance. Rather, he finds God working in indirect, often oblique fashion, in many dimensions of human existence. Finding himself disenchanted with the ecumenical movement and much church worship, he wants to concentrate in a focussed manner on the witness of Jesus to the enormous resources of God's kingdom, in which abundance is God's gift to those most in need. He writes:

It seems to me that much traditional Christian theology nobody needs to know. Indeed the question can be raised: why do we need theological statements at all? The answer might be that theological statements are coded instructions for various kinds of activity . . . I am persuaded that the Christian community has a capacity for acting in the Jesus manner when help is needed. Not to do the same things as other helpers provide, and certainly not to share the confusion and incompetence often felt by professional helpers; but to exercise its own Christian skills, not only or chiefly for the benefit of its members but for the healing of the sick world (p. 75).

Re-examining Methodist theology

There are, however, other voices. Three books published by Epworth Press in its *Groundwork* series – *Groundwork of Philosophy of Religion* by David A. Pailin (1986), *Groundwork of Christian Ethics* by Richard G. Jones (1984) and *Groundwork of Theology* by John Stacey (1977, revised 1984) – provide valuable evidence.

All three volumes, though revealing openness to other Christian traditions and a willingness to use ideas which they have generated, are especially attentive to issues defined and answers proposed in discussions among contemporary British scholars.

David A. Pailin

Pailin, who provides the widest background, can aptly introduce the content of these volumes. His study is both remarkably broad and exceptionally well ordered. Attention is given to traditional issues in philosophy of religion, but with a distinct awareness of the overlap of philosophy of religion and theology (p. 3).

As the chapter titles indicate, the discussion is structured around the theme of faith: for example, 'Faith, Religion and Philosophy'; 'Faith, Culture and Doctrine'; 'Faith, History and Revelation'; 'Faith and the Attributes of God'; 'Faith, History and the Existence of God'; 'Faith, Death and Immortality'; 'Faith, Morality and Experience'; and 'Faith and Religious Language'.

The approach throughout is irenic and acknowledgment of contributions from many sources is typical. Consistently, the author indicates a range of valid options in regard to each issue and leaves space for the reader to draw his or her own conclusions.

The issues are developed in terms of prevailing British philosophical discussion along with process philosophy. The book is a fine introduction to recent philosophy of religion and is presented with unusual sensitivity to the religious importance of the issues. It is not and should not be specifically Methodist. Although it breathes Methodist air, it is representative of responsible intellectual engagement by a person deeply involved in his intellectual discipline.

Pailin's theological employment of his philosophical background has been expressed for four decades and may be found, for instance, in his chapter, 'The Poet of Salvation' in the volume, *Freedom and Grace*, edited by Ivor H. Jones and Kenneth B. Wilson (Epworth Press 1988), in his article on 'The Doctrine of the Atonement' (*Epworth Review*, September 1991), and in his book, *The Anthropological Character of Theology* (CUP 1990). In exploring the meaning of salvation, Pailin once again looks thoroughly and clearly at the inherited meanings and the contemporary difficulty of simply repeating them.

There is an analytical acuteness in his exploration and a rigorous effort to ask what from the past may be retained. His answer is a continuation of Protestant liberalism. He is especially anxious to affirm the significance of human being. The two important words are 'significance' and 'being'. The effort is more to deal with human finiteness than with traditional interpretations of human sinfulness.

Pailin calls upon Process philosophical theology to reinterpret the understanding of God who is actively present in the creation. Following Alfred North Whitehead, Charles Hartshorne and Schubert M. Ogden he wants to set aside 'classical' notions of God as the One, self-sufficient, unmoved, and permanent reality. He moves to a Process understanding of salvation as preservation. According to this, God saves the good in the world as it passes into the immediacy of his own life, and salvation is the expression of the creative freedom of both God and human beings.

Pailin is a thinker who uses philosophy to prepare the ground for theology and understands theology as a rigorous discipline which answers issues which have been raised by philosophical analysis.

Richard G. Jones

Richard G. Jones in his *Groundwork of Christian Ethics* exhibits a special interest in social ethics. After an initial discussion of biblical ethical teaching, which he finds complex and inconsistent, he concludes that 'The error which has been haunting the whole of the discussion so far in this chapter is that of assuming that the Bible on its own is a sufficient authority or source for Christian ethics. It never has been, and never will be.'[4]

Since the Bible cannot function as the single authority or guide, it is necessary to utilize tradition, reason and experience. (Though not an exclusively Methodist formula, this accords with the so-called quadrilateral used by John Wesley and is typical of Methodists.) It is not made clear, however, whether there is any order of priority among these sources or how conflicts between them are to be resolved. In practice, reason seems to play the most crucial role and the importance of 'scientific data' is stressed.

Jones explores a variety of ethical problems, including war and violence, sexuality and marriage, human rights, medical ethics, technology and life-styles. In each case, a number of options are presented and contributions from various disciplines are surveyed. The range and fairness of the presentations are noteworthy, but no sharp conclusions are drawn.

In his concluding chapter, the author mentions points which should receive special attention in arriving at ethical decisions: set out the biblical traditions; outline the various Christian traditions; explain the teaching of your own tradition; respect those disciplines which help with detailed information about the issue; and leave people to make up their own minds.[5] The book itself exhibits careful attention to the first two and the last two points. What is missing is any development of the teaching of his own tradition.

In a short reference to Methodism (pp. 73–75), Jones expresses distress that, for much of the time, it has been over-preoccupied with individual piety and has failed to address structural faults in the social system. Since we are concerned with tradition, we note that, in this case, lack of involvement in a particular tradition leads to a treatment of ethics as a free-standing intellectual discipline and to a lack of a clear standpoint from which various options may be evaluated. In the end, one has worked around the points on the compass, but there is no needle to provide direction. The book is to be commended, however, for the range of its awareness and for the attention it gives to different Christian ethical positions.

John Stacey

Of special interest to us in our general discussion is John Stacey's *Groundwork of Theology*. The book began life as a textbook for Methodist Local Preachers, and Stacey wrote as a Methodist for Methodists. To the extent that this treatment of Christian doctrine has been endorsed by the church, it may be regarded as, in some sense, representative of Methodism's current theological position. At the same time, and this is typical of the Methodist Church, it is a single person's interpretation and should be understood as a guide and not as a prescription of doctrine.

In spirit and content the book is characteristic of Methodism. It focusses throughout on theology as servant to preaching, acknowledges a debt to a wide range of Christian traditions, and gives due attention to the evangelical doctrines. If belonging to a particular tradition means that there are others, whose fundamental standpoint one shares, with whom one argues and from whom one learns in a special way, then this is a Methodist theological expression. Among Methodists, there may be disagreement about particular points of doctrine, but a ground for discussion has been set and an invitation to dialogue has been issued.

Stacey, beginning with a discussion of 'religion', assumes a universal religious sensibility which is given expression through specific religious traditions. Christianity is one expression of religious commitment and, as a Christian, Stacey discusses religious faith from that perspective, but with acknowledgment of and respect for non-Christian traditions.

Christian theology is centred in Jesus Christ, for Jesus is the source and the end of Christian understanding of God, human nature, the church and the totality of history. Access to Jesus Christ comes through the Bible [88], tradition, reason and Christian experience. (Once again this four-fold formula for the source of theological understanding is used.)

> **88.** (Rejection of biblical scholarship can lead to) the danger that we shall be found excluding the Lord of truth from his own dominions. The Lord of scripture is also the Lord of historical, literary and theological truth and to oppose the search for the latter on the ground of loyalty to the former is to imply a schizophrenic God. But God is not so divided and his truth is indivisible.
>
> *Source*: John Stacey, *Groundwork of Theology*, Epworth Press 1984, p. 38.

It is significant that in the opening section, where religion and theology are discussed, equal footing is also given to the theme of 'Theology and Living'. This is a clear acknowledgment of the practical import of theology. Theology is not simply an abstract interpretation of intellectual themes. While it is an intellectual endeavour, the total person and total community are involved in theological exploration. In this way, theology underwrites practical life, and the end of theological inquiry is a more adequate preaching of the Christian gospel and a more complete embodiment of Christian virtue.

In Part II the central doctrines of Christian faith are explored, beginning with the doctrine of God. The most important characteristics of God are succinctly expressed: God is creator, personal, holy, righteous, singular, eternal, spirit, almighty, father, love and mystery [89]. Each of these perceptions, which are basically shared by the entire Christian movement, is clearly and straightforwardly discussed.

> **89.** We have to be *aware* that when we speak of God as creator, personal, holy and so forth we are using 'God' as a kind of sign, a piece of shorthand, for the God whom no words can adequately describe. We are speaking of a Being (with a capital 'B' for his supremacy) simply because we cannot speak of Being in our language. On this assumption we can go ahead and talk about God.
>
> *Source*: John Stacey, *Groundwork of Theology*, Epworth Press 1984, p. 84.

Stacey's interest in preaching and the practical implications of theology is exhibited by the 'Present Considerations' which conclude the discussion of each doctrine. In these sections, he relates his exposition to contemporary mindsets, problems, and critical sensibilities. For instance, with regard to the doctrine of God, how do we deal with secularization, the problems of evil and suffering, and mangled notions of God? By raising these questions quite explicitly, Stacey is challenging preachers to present the Christian understanding of God realistically and effectively.

Christology is central in this presentation. The discussion of Jesus Christ intends to be faithful to biblical sources and attention is given to the person of Jesus. Nevertheless, the central emphasis, in keeping with evangelical traditions, is upon Jesus' death and resurrection.

The initial discussion is completed with the doctrines of the Holy Spirit [90] and the Trinity. The

> **90.** The doctrine of the Holy Spirit comes out of the New Testament. It is not imposed upon it. Only if this process has been accepted as basic to all talk about the Holy Spirit in the New Testament can the titles below, describing what is known of the Holy Spirit, be used.
>
> *Source*: John Stacey, *Groundwork of Theology*, Epworth Press 1984, p. 161.

comprehensiveness of the Spirit's presence, as attested in the Old and New Testaments, in Jesus Christ, in the life of the church and in individual Christian existence, is emphasized.

Specifically, the Holy Spirit is defined as the Spirit of God, the Spirit of Christ, and the Spirit of truth. The central conviction of Christian experience is that, when the Holy Spirit is experienced, believers are experiencing God the Father and Jesus Christ.

With the experience of God as Creator/Father, in Jesus Christ and in the Holy Spirit, the ingredients are drawn together to formulate the doctrine of the Trinity. In regard to Christian affirmation of the Trinity, Stacey comments, 'It was a matter of setting rules for talking. The single word "God" was not adequate on its own, for it did not convey the reality of the threefold experience that the early Christians enjoyed. Father – Son – Holy Spirit did.'[6]

Following the exploration of the doctrine of God in its fullest Trinitarian terms, the exposition turns to 'Humanity and its Salvation'. In many ways this theme has been present from the beginning: because of a need to support the responsibility of preaching, because of a desire to link theology and life, and because of an acceptance of the general Wesleyan commitment to 'offer Christ'.

Human complicity in sin, the blemishing of the image of God, makes necessary an understanding of salvation. The primary emphasis is upon salvation as the work of a gracious God. The 'pattern of salvation' – some Methodists have called this 'the order of salvation' – moves through conversion, justification, redemption, adoption, regeneration, reconciliation, and sanctification. This salvation is free for all people and to all people [91].

Discussions of the kingdom of God and the church complete the body of the presentation. The kingdom is inaugurated by Jesus, as present reality and as future hope. God's reign is established and is sure; upon this foundation Christian life is built.

The church is for: worship, prayer, preaching and teaching, celebrating the sacraments, ministry, mis-

---

> **91.** The Wesleys, and Methodism after them, were Arminians, and their Arminianism made them evangelicals, not in the party sense in which the word has subsequently been used, but in the sense that salvation was 'for every soul of man'. Methodism's answer to hard predestination was clear enough.
>
> > Thy undistinguishing regard
> > Was cast on Adam's fallen race;
> > For all thou hast in Christ prepared
> > Sufficient, sovereign, saving grace.
>
> *Source*: John Stacey, *Groundwork of Theology*, Epworth Press 1984, p. 197.

sion and unity [92]. The commentary on these topics reflects both general Christian consensus and Methodist agreement. It is important that the list ends with unity, a theme which British Methodism has been stressing for the last half of the twentieth century. It is also a goal which it has struggled for and been frustrated by, but which still stands as a lively hope. 'We are dealing here not with "our unhappy divisions" but with an outrageous denial of God'.[7]

> **92.** This means that the church is not first a fellowship for the religious, nor a service agency for the unfortunate, nor a counselling centre for the disturbed, nor a talking shop for theologians. The church is first the community that lives by faith, hope and love, and all for God, because that is how it was with Jesus.
>
> *Source*: John Stacey, *Groundwork of Theology*, Epworth Press 1984, p. 265.

In an appendix, the author provides specific Methodist materials for each of the doctrines discussed. Consistently used are the Apostles' Creed, the Nicene Creed, John Wesley's *Explanatory Notes on the New Testament*, Wesley's sermons, the *Methodist Service Book*, and the *Methodist Hymn Book*. It is important that the Methodist sources reinforce the general discussion and do not provide any distinctive interpretation.

The book concludes by focussing on Methodist

preachers. This is appropriate, granted its immediate purpose, but it also reflects the longstanding Methodist conviction that theology, fundamentally, is in the service of proclamation.

What appears to be the case, both in this presentation and in British Methodism in general, is that distinctively Wesleyan or Methodist theological interests have yielded to more general and commonly accepted Christian theological themes. There is faithfulness to ecumenical creeds and historic doctrines of Protestant and Anglican Christianity, with particular interest in scripture and preaching. Little explicit emphasis is given to such traditional Methodist doctrines as sanctification. In the course of this change, special Wesleyan and Methodist theological traditions play no significant role. Their nurture in Methodism has made its present representatives appreciative of and conformed to commonly affirmed Christian doctrine.

We have spent much time with Stacey's book because it is representative of contemporary British Methodist theological interests. Yet, as a systematic theology, it reflects a limited stream in Methodism. Indeed, while there have been systematic statements by Methodists in Great Britain, writings focussed on particular doctrines or dealing with particular occasions as they arise, have been far more typical.

Within British Methodism, biblical study has continued to be important. Even a short list of significant scholars makes this clear: C. K. Barrett, Morna D. Hooker, James D. G. Dunn, Kenneth Grayston, I. Howard Marshall, and W. David Stacey. Though theologically far from unanimous, they reflect the continuing importance of biblical rootedness to the Methodist tradition.

An evangelical perspective

There is a small book which, with admirable brevity and clarity, sets forth the primary theological emphases within the Methodist tradition from a more evangelical perspective. The book is Michael J. Townsend's *Our Tradition of Faith* which was published by Epworth Press in 1980.

Michael Townsend begins his book, which is written as a refresher course for preachers, by discussing 'The Possibility of Having Doctrinal Standards' [93]. After looking at the formal standards in the official church statements of 1936 and 1975, he quotes Professor C. K. Barrett, who says that the Methodist tradition has attempted to 'secure loyalty to fundamental truths' rather than to define the full range of doctrine.

Townsend then discusses several contemporary issues, such as diversity of scriptural witness, the impact of cultural diversity, the meaning of revelation, and the character of doctrinal truth. Of central importance is his emphasis upon revelation being expressed primarily in a person – Jesus Christ – and only secondarily in propositions which fill out who that person is. Recognizing the ecumenical character of contemporary Christian life and thought, he especially asks the question: what are some of the contributions Methodism holds in trust for the larger body of Christ?

---

93. The Church will be wise these days to take its doctrinal standards as guides rather than chains. Many writers have used the image of 'exploration' for theology, and there is a good deal to commend this. But we are not explorers without chart or compass, lost in unknown territory. Martin Thornton has a most telling passage in this connection: 'The map is not the country any more than the doctrine of the Trinity is God, but properly used they are both accurate guides: the map will lead you through the country and the creed will inspire and interpret prayer in the light of revelation.'

Source: Michael J. Townsend, *Our Tradition of Faith*, Epworth Press 1980, p. 40.

In the Methodist tradition, Townsend says, there are four major doctrinal emphases:

All men can be saved
All men can be saved by grace through faith
All men may know that they are saved
All men may be saved to the uttermost.

He especially comments upon the meaning of

salvation for contemporary people, which he locates in the word 'liberation'. Then he explores the meaning of assurance, or knowing that we are saved, putting primary stress upon relationship with God and God's faithfulness in relationship. Finally, he concentrates on sanctification or being saved to the uttermost, expounding it in terms of the thorough love of God with heart, mind, strength and will which that relationship makes possible. Throughout, Townsend offers a cautious, traditional view by utilizing a wide range of theological commentary. He is conversant with both scriptural studies and historical Methodist teachings and attempts to relate this received past to the living present.

Ecumenical horizons

Methodism, since the time of John Wesley, has been generously affirming of other Christian traditions. It has recognized an indebtedness to the historical sweep of developments from the early ecumenical centuries, to the Protestant Reformation, to Roman Catholicism, to its Anglican context. Methodists, recognizing their mission as part of the total life of the Christian movement, have endorsed the practices and achievements of other Christians.

From the end of the nineteenth century through the first third of the twentieth century, Methodists were chiefly concerned with unity among themselves. With the formation of the Methodist Church in Great Britain in 1932, however, the possibility of a more inclusive unity gripped their attention, and British Methodist theology was decisively shaped by this enlarged vision [94].

A broader vision

One indication of this broader vision was evident in the expansion of scholarly interest to other Christian traditions. Of chief significance was seminal work done in the exploration of the thought of Martin Luther by Philip S. Watson (b. 1909) and E. Gordon Rupp (1910–1986).

---

94. One day in the last century, two old men sat together on a park bench in the city of Birmingham. The one was a Methodist supernumerary (I have the story from his grandson). The other was John Cardinal Newman. They talked about what the church is and who be thereof. Newman took the other's umbrella and poked in the dust a circle on the ground and said, 'I think you have to get the circumference right.' The old Methodist took his umbrella back and poked a single hole in the centre and said, 'Ah, we think that you must begin with the centre, and if you get that right the circumference will look after itself.' Well, it is an apocryphal and perhaps implausible tale but it may have a truth about Methodism.

Source: E. Gordon Rupp, 'The Doctrine of the Church at the Reformation' in Dow Kirkpatrick (ed), *The Doctrine of the Church*, Abingdon 1964, p. 78.

Philip Watson taught theology in English Methodist theological colleges and at Garrett Theological Seminary in the United States. His major study was *Let God Be God* (1949), an investigation of the sovereignty of God in the thought of Martin Luther. Luther, Watson argued, effected a 'Copernican revolution' in realigning theology from anthropocentrism to God-centredness. The centrality of God's action was further stated in *The Concept of Grace* (1959) and also in the introduction to the collection of Wesley writings which he edited, *the Message of the Wesleys* (1964).

Gordon Rupp, a masterful historian, both as researcher and as stylish presenter, also contributed to the study of Martin Luther with his *The Righteousness of God* (1953) and in studies of the Reformation, both on the continent and in Great Britain, in his books *Principalities and Powers* (1952) and *Just Men* (1977). Drawing these themes together with his own heritage, he wrote *Methodism in Relation to the Protestant Tradition* (1954). In addition, he produced a study of Thomas Jackson, a nineteenth-century Methodist editor and historian. Rupp participated in bi-lateral conversations of the World Methodist Council with Roman Catholicism and with the Lutheran World Federation and contributed to Methodism's further participation in general ecumenical life.

Following in this area of large ecumenical study, Peter Stephens has written two studies of Ulrich Zwingli (1986, 1992) but also has maintained an interest in his heritage by writing a report on Methodism in Europe (c. 1982) and an earlier book of sermons, *Faith And Love* (1971).

Journals

Of special importance in the continuation of the Methodist tradition and as an ongoing influence in shaping that tradition have been the theological periodicals *The London and Holborn Review* and *Epworth Review*. These two journals have for a century been a means of communication within the tradition, a conveyance of personages and life in the tradition, and an enricher of the tradition by reaching beyond Methodism and guiding discussion on a number of issues such as preaching, atonement, the convincing power of Christian faith, and personality and theology. Especially in the last decade, and under the editorship of John Stacey, the *Epworth Review* has been a stimulating journal of high order and a promoter of discussion. The contributions of these journals have helped to keep the Methodist Connexion self-consciously alive.

Ecumenical theology

There is an interesting similarity and contrast between two contemporary British Methodist theologians, Rupert E. Davies (1909–1994) and Geoffrey Wainwright (b. 1939). These men share a keen interest in the Wesleys and their teaching but neither evidences comparable enthusiasm for intervening Methodist theological developments. Both have a strong and thoroughgoing ecumenical commitment and are concerned about the relating of historical creeds to the present.

Yet there is a contrast for, on the one hand, Davies aims to interpret the creeds in order to make them meaningful for contemporary people with modern

mindsets, while Wainwright's effort is to lead contemporary people, even with their modern mindsets, into an understanding of the creeds. To put the contrast tersely: on balance, Davies wants to bring the creeds to contemporary people; Wainwright wants to bring contemporary people back to the creeds. Both are committed to the importance of the creeds, but the difference in their approaches has profound significance.

The work of Rupert Davies

Davies was a scholar, a teacher, a President of the Methodist Conference, a circuit superintendent, a member of the Faith and Order Committee of the World Council of Churches, a resolute champion of church unity, and for forty years an interpreter of Methodism both to Methodists and to those outside of Methodism [95].

---

95. Methodism, since Methodist Union, has experienced many changes, some forced upon it, some actively and consciously willed by its leaders and people . . . Many of the changes have been in the direction of assimilation to other churches . . . many have been designed to preserve and strengthen its distinctive characteristics. The result so far, it can be argued (but also presumably disputed), has been to maintain the essentials of Methodist teaching and spirituality (though not always at a deep enough level), while dispensing with many of the formulae and activities in which they used to be clothed, and to fit the Methodist people in some measure for the reciprocal sharing of spiritual treasure with other Christians.

Source: Rupert Davies, 'Since 1932' in Rupert Davies, A. Raymond George and Gordon Rupp (eds), *A History of the Methodist Church in Great Britain*, vol. 3, Epworth Press 1983, p. 390.

Davies set the context of his work in his book *Religious Authority in an Age of Doubt* (1968). 'The age in which we live is likely to go down in history as the age which finally cast off all religious authority. It is with the fundamental changes in the mental attitude of our time, and especially with the decline of religious authority, that this book is mainly concerned.'[8] Throughout, Davies' theological interpretation consistently intends to help Christian faith tackle this problem.

Standing side by side with this modern intellectual situation is the reality of ecumenism. Davies is convinced that there is and must be progress in seeking unity among Christians. And in ecumenical discussions he sees a growing awareness of complementarity rather than contradiction in regard to basic doctrine and efforts at mutual acceptance and support rather than conflict and antagonism. Agreement is being realized especially in regard to eucharist, ministry and baptism.[9]

His own approach, coming in large part from his Methodist tradition, is centred in Jesus Christ. Jesus Christ is the unique and supreme authority for life. '[This] means that there is no going behind Christ for further information about God, that in Christ is everything, implicitly or explicitly, that we need to be told about God and his purposes for the world and for us . . .'[10]

The authority of Jesus Christ is found in the immediate experience of God in Christ transmitted by the Holy Spirit to the life of believers. Faith incorporates one into the fellowship of the church [96].

---

96. The implications for thought make up what is called Christian theology, and take the form of doctrines and doctrinal teachings. The Christian works these out, assisted and guided (though not infallibly) by the Holy Spirit (as he firmly believes), by the use of his reason, by his spiritual insight (which is the best name for the Inner Light, since it does not imply, though it does not deny, that there is something of God in every man) and by his conscience. He does this in the context of the worshipping and teaching life of the Church, and thus enters into its agelong heritage of theological thought and controversy.

Source: Rupert E. Davies, Religious Authority in an Age of Doubt, Epworth Press 1968, p. 218.

In What Methodists Believe (1976) Davies begins, once again, with the affirmation of the centrality of Jesus Christ. 'Jesus Christ is the centre and mainspring of Christian faith. To say what Christians believe without putting him in the forefront of everything that is said would be like trying to play a game of cricket without having a batsman at the wicket.'[11]

Davies then moves to a statement of beliefs that are common to Christians; and thus a large part of his answer to the question, 'What do Methodists believe?' consists in saying what all Christians believe.

The structure of this book, once again, reveals Davies' concern for the contemporary mind. In his discussion of Jesus Christ, God, the Holy Spirit and the Church he continues to ask, how can these doctrines be meaningfully interpreted for contemporary people? The discussion is ecumenical, clear and straightforward, and the only explicit reference to John Wesley concerns the Christian's lifestyle as a holy vocation [97]. While acknowledging distortions and misinterpretations, Davies nevertheless asserts, 'Yet there is an important truth behind Wesley's teaching on this matter. Christianity is not meant to be a half-and-half affair, but asks of us that we should set before ourselves nothing less than the highest possible standard, that is, the standard of perfect love.'[12]

---

97. Its [John Wesley's conversion] immediate effect on John Wesley – and, at much the same time on his brother Charles – was to divert him from an intense absorption in the state of this own soul to an overwhelming urge to make known to other people what he had discovered for himself. This was the dominant motive for his nationwide and lifelong mission.

Source: Rupert E. Davies, What Methodists Believe, Mowbray 1976, p. 95.

In the second part of the book Davies considers 'The Methodist Approach to this Common Christian Faith.' In discussing Wesley, he sets him within his own time and makes clear his unusual sensitivity not only to personal religious experience but also to the general condition of the people. Davies is fully aware of Wesley's emotionalism and of the difficulties in the emphases of some of his sermons, such as his stress upon the torments of hell, but he emphasizes that Wesley spent an immense amount of his time and energy attempting to deal with the physical and material needs of the underprivileged and that he organized his followers very effectively into groups that nurtured Christian living.

Davies expresses unhappiness over the failure of the attempts at union between the Methodist Church and the Church of England in 1969 and 1972. He believes that the cause was right and that hope for union must continue. He discusses Methodism from the perspective of this continuing hope, emphasizing what he thinks are important potential contributions of Methodism [98]: the dual tradition in worship, that is, liturgical sensitivity and spontaneous freedom; Methodism's special concern for social issues; the universal scope of the gospel as free for all and to all; the role of laity in significant ministry; and Methodism's emphasis on personal – not individual but personal – relationship with God. All of these qualities Methodism can bring to a united church.

---

98. Methodism has much to learn from other Christians, it is evident, as well as something, perhaps, to teach them. It holds that only in a united Church can the truths committed to each separate denomination be seen in their true context, and the errors to which each denomination has been prone be seen as such and removed.

Source: Rupert E. Davies, *What Methodists Believe*, Mowbray 1976, p. 112.

In 1987 Davies published *Making Sense of the Creeds*. His position is clearly stated. 'On the assumption that the creeds, in their own way, assert universal Christian belief, we can dig beneath the words and thought-systems of the ancient Graeco-Roman world to discover what the creeds are basically saying, and then try to reassert the truths thus discovered in language which is intelligible and credible to modern minds.'[13][99]

Pursuing this intention he goes on to discuss God the Father almighty, Jesus Christ, the Holy Spirit, human salvation, and the church. His interpretations for the current situation may be illustrated by his discussion of the person of Jesus Christ. He insists that 'Jesus was, quite simply, a man – a man with superb gifts of mind and spirit, a man in close communion with his Father in heaven, but a man . . . If so, this was the way that the divine son of God chose to reveal the love of God, to fulfil his mission and to offer salvation to the world; and it was his faithfulness, courage and endurance in following this way that God the Father honoured and accepted by raising him from the dead.'[14]

---

99. We have seen (or haven't we?) that the Nicene Creed, which is the centrepiece of credal confessions, needs some reinterpretation for our times; that reformulation at certain points would not come amiss; that there are serious omissions which need to be repaired; and that there are 'new' truths which are not recognized.

Source: Rupert E. Davies, *Making Sense of the Creeds*, Epworth Press 1987, p. 84.

Davies wants to keep the creeds and he believes that the great communions of Christendom do also, for the creeds still witness to great principles of the faith, 'albeit, to us, sometimes obscurely'.[15] Yet, however highly we may regard them, they cannot in the end do more than mark a stage – a long and important one – in the exploration of Christian faith, and in apprehension of the truth as truth is in Jesus; they do not give the final solutions of every problem. Nowadays, moreover, the church faces not so much splits within itself (though the danger of those is not removed) as the splitting away of human society from the church.[16]

To reiterate the most important general point, Davies takes both his Wesleyan heritage and the creedal foundations of the church with great seriousness. But, as a contemporary person who wants to speak to contemporary people, he believes that this must be done by an ongoing reinterpretation of the creeds in order to make them intelligible and helpful.

The work of Geoffrey Wainwright

Wainwright is a British Methodist theologian who has spent the major part of his active teaching career outside Great Britain, first in Cameroon, then after a time at The Queen's College, Birmingham, at Union Theological Seminary in New York, and for the last decade and a half at the Divinity School, Duke University. His career has been marked by the wide relationships he has established with many Christian communions, while also consciously maintaining deep rootedness in the particularities of the Wesleyan heritage.

His first major book, *Eucharist and Eschatology* (1971) already shows this dual interest in the Wesleyan tradition and the widest ecumenical theological developments. His study imbibed deeply of the theological commitments of both the Wesleys and of Charles Wesley's hymnody. At the same time, it shows constant awareness of theological discussion among Roman Catholics, Eastern Orthodox, and Protestant traditions.

In 1980 Wainwright published a systematic theology entitled *Doxology*. Developing what he calls 'a pictorial method of presentation', he argues that worship is the context in which Christian vision comes to clarity and within which Christian understanding can be most adequately developed.

Beginning with the substance of theology in his discussion of God, Christ, the Holy Spirit and the church, Wainwright moves first to the means of theological transmission: scripture, creeds, hymns, worship and doctrine and then, finally, to the context of the church and the world as expressed in ecumenism, culture and ethics. Once again, his own ecumenical awareness is exceptionally broad as he utilizes resources from the full spread of the Christian heritage.

Wainwright's work is christologically centred but it is developed in trinitarian terms. There is emphasis upon full-orbed interpretation of God who is the beginning and the end, the alpha and the omega. This God is decisively revealed in Jesus Christ and what is revealed is the triune God. In addition, there is a primary emphasis upon personal relationships, that is, the relationship of God to human beings and the relationship of human beings to God. This personal relationship is exhibited in worship, and particularly in the sacraments.

The implications of both worship and theology for ecumenism and liturgical revision constitute a major part of *Doxology*. Common worship provides the basis for dialogue among the major Christian traditions. Called by God's grace to communion with God, the richness of this communion means that theology is always in search of more adequate statement. Jesus Christ remains the norm for worship and theology, but there is an openness to God's revelation, an openness which can lead to fuller understanding of God's glory through Christian dialogue rooted in communion with God.

For the past decade and a half Wainwright's concentration has been upon ecumenical matters as he has engaged in dialogue with other Christian traditions. In a distinctive way he has continued to carry a deep sense of his own Wesleyan and Methodist tradition, always attempting to bring its special emphases into creative relationship with emphases from other traditions [100].

A singular contribution may be found in the Faith and Order document prepared for the World Council of Churches in 1982. This document, often referred to as 'The Lima Text', has the title of *Baptism, Eucharist and Ministry*, and Wainwright was one of its principal authors. The three themes – baptism, eucharist and ministry – have been among the most difficult for the various churches to achieve a common understanding. Clear definition and happy agreement created what some have called 'the decade of BEM'.

From 1983 until 1990 Faith and Order continued its work, producing a 100-page booklet entitled *Confessing the One Faith*. This document, which has been commended to the churches for study, represents an effort to ground Christian unity in the truth of the gospel. There is movement from common

100. Allowing for the lapse of two hundred years, there is a close correspondence between the classic ecumenical movement and the profile of John Wesley that informed Methodists, and others, would recognize. Wesley's vision, program, and praxis were marked by the following six principal features. First, he looked to the *Scriptures* as the primary and abiding testimony to the redemptive work of God in Christ. Second, he was utterly committed to the ministry of *evangelism*, where the gospel was to be preached to every creature and needed only to be accepted in faith. Third, he valued with respect the Christian Tradition and the doctrine of the Church a *generous orthodoxy* wherein theological opinions might vary as long as they were consistent with the apostolic teaching. Fourth, he expected *sanctification* to show itself in the moral earnestness and loving deeds of the believers. Fifth, he manifested and encouraged a *social concern* that was directed toward the neediest of neighbours. Sixth, he found in the *Lord's Supper* a sacramental sign of the fellowship graciously bestowed by the Triune God and the responsive sacrifice of praise and thanksgiving on the part of those who will glorify God and enjoy him forever. These are the features which must be strengthened in contemporary Methodism, if we are to maintain our historic identity, speak with a significant voice on the ecumenical scene, and keep on a recognizably Christian track as the ways diverge.

Source: Geoffrey Wainwright, *Methodists in Dialog*, Abingdon 1995, pp. 283–84.

acknowledgment in worship to common effort to explore and express Christian understanding. It needs to be said that the unity sought is not easily won. Rather, fundamental agreement is always balanced with basic differences. What has been won are common positions in regard to some basic doctrines, the development of extreme good will and mutual affirmation among various ecclesial bodies.

In 'Continuing a Methodist Voice', the conclusion to his *Methodists in Dialog*, Wainwright acknowledges that the Methodist movement has been wider than the Wesleys; nevertheless he holds that 'Methodism's dominant standards have been Wesleyan.' Hence, 'a Wesleyan renewal in doctrine and theology involves the affirmation, with Wesley, of the great tenets of the Church's belief: the transcendent Three-One God, Father, Son and Holy Spirit, one in deity and worship, three persons mutually indwelling and perfectly cooperating; the divine creation of the world and the vocation of humankind to holiness and happiness; the incarnation and atoning work of God the Son in Jesus Christ our Lord; the Spirit of God, who is the source of all truth, renewal and communion; the need of fallen human kind to repent and believe the gospel; the divine provision of grace through word and sacrament; the summons to love of God and neighbour; the institution and gathering of a Church whose divine fellowship transcends time and space; the promise of a final judgment and victory, where all the redeemed will share in glorifying and enjoying God for ever.'[17]

Wainwright sees the way forward in ecumenical dialogue to be grounded in a reappropriation of the meaning of the early, ecumenical creeds, especially the Nicene-Constantinopolitan Creed.[18] This creed still retains its validity and centrality for ongoing achievement of Christian unity and it has been adopted by the plenary of the Commission on Faith and Order as its foundation document for continuing work.

A chief issue for Wainwright which demonstrates this need for retaining classical language is the doctrine of the Trinity. Modern discussions of the Trinity have moved towards functional descriptions; Wainwright, on the other hand, is convinced that it is necessary to use person language and insists upon the traditional formulation of Father, Son and Holy Spirit.[19]

There is clear awareness that codifications of Christian faith have been historically conditioned and that there are differing interpretations even within a common Christian tradition. Nevertheless, the Nicene-Constantinopolitan Creed provides the strongest foundation for continuing construction of doctrine. Many factors make the establishment of new bases for ecumenical agreement extremely difficult. But, he contends, we have an ancient and adequate base, and it should be fully used.

With Wainwright, we have the most complete

affirmation of classical Christian doctrine among contemporary British Methodist theologians. Such an affirmation, he is convinced, is mandatory at this time when these classical formulations are being challenged. What is not so clear is the relation of Wainwright to contemporary British Methodist theology, for he cuts across the dominant stream. His absence from Britain may accentuate differences, but both his heritage and his ongoing interest make the consideration of his position important.

Ecumenical response

The response of the British Methodist Church to *Baptism, Eucharist and Ministry*, prepared by their Faith and Order commission, is a good indicator of where British Methodist theology presently places itself within the spectrum of ecumenical thought.

In an extended reply, the emphases which Methodism has maintained are indicated with clarity and deep appreciation. Typically, there is little mention of John Wesley and no explicit references to the Methodist tradition. But what is affirmed is in clear continuity with what has characterized Methodism through its existence and in its recent statements.

This response makes clear that contemporary British Methodism is both aware of present theological problems and open to ongoing work on doctrinal agreements, clarifications, fresh statements and new convergences. Thus, while the authority of scripture is acknowledged in principle, significant questions are asked. What type of authority is this? How is it to be applied? How is it to be related to the continuing work of the Holy Spirit? All of these matters are left vague by BEM. But the issue of how the principle of biblical authority can be applied remains crucial. Not unexpectedly, British Methodism's response to BEM calls for more attention to be paid to the cultural context of theology and church structures.

The response also raises questions – and here Methodism's evangelical ethos is influential – about the sacramental efficacy of baptism. Does the rite of baptism itself incorporate one into Christ? Wash away sins? Bring new birth? Or does the rite 'signify' that

this is an important element in Christian life? Throughout, however, there is clear emphasis upon the initiative and work of God, for 'the efficacy of the sacraments depends upon God and not upon any supposed automatism in the rite'.[20]

Again, the response expresses reservations about BEM's suggestion that infant baptism and believer baptism are 'equivalent alternatives'. There may be a fundamental difference here with radical implications for ecclesiology. It seems unlikely, in fact, that an issue which has separated churches can easily be resolved in a united church, and a word of caution is perhaps appropriate.

Moreover, the status and role of the minister presiding at the eucharist requires clarification. The Methodist tradition has emphasized, in the 'Deed of Union' and in the Conference Statement on ordination in 1974, that the offering is made by the whole people of God and is presided over by the minister. The minister neither adds an essential element nor is the sacrament specifically activated by the minister's presence. The minister, for Methodists, is representative of the people and is not different in kind.

The Methodist response places strong emphasis – and this is specially important – on preaching as a mode of grace or as a vehicle for conveying the divine Word. This must be kept in counter-balance with emphasis on the eucharist. Methodists have been nourished by preaching services, and with this claim divine initiative and freedom are maintained in distinctively Methodist fashion. Divine operation is found in preaching as well as in the sacraments.

The status and authenticity of Methodist ministry is further supported by a profound resistance to BEM's claim of episcopal ministry in apostolic succession. Methodists are seeking for mutual recognition of different forms of ministry as authentic and the rejection of any hint that non-episcopal ministry is in any way deprived or inferior. They are asking from others for a recognition they are willing to give.

In this response to a general ecumenical statement, British Methodism reveals some of the most prized parts of its inheritance. Along with ecumenical openness there is continuing emphasis on its characteristic modes of organized life and mission. Back in 1959, however, Gordon Rupp warned against too strong an attachment to our Methodist past [101].

> 101. The whole life and history of Methodism constitute a treasure of the Church, but let us not idolize it or suppose that it must go on in history for all time. Let us realize that in history Churches have their day and cease to be. If it ever happens that Methodism becomes a part of the past, like the seven Churches of Asia Minor, the Spirit will still be speaking to the Churches in other ways, and giving bounteous gifts. It may be that we are at the beginning of Church history; it may be that what God waits to do for the Church in the future will far eclipse all the great things all the Churches have seen and enjoyed.
>
> *Source*: Gordon Rupp, 'The Future of the Methodist Tradition', *The London Quarterly and Holborn Review*, July 1959, p. 273.

Another dimension

Contemporary British Methodist theology is diverse. This is obvious from the previous discussion. How to find the trunkline, if such a thing exists, is difficult to determine. But among important representatives is a group of theologians who bring both keen awareness of the Methodist tradition and the contemporary setting of religious and intellectual life. In the volume *Freedom and Grace*, edited by Ivor H. Jones and Kenneth B. Wilson (1988), nine Methodist scholars represent a high quality of thought. 'The purpose of the publication is to enable Methodists to share in our reflections with the expectation that this may promote a fuller discussion of the Methodist tradition.'[21]

Each of these scholars reflects, from the vantage point of their Methodist heritage, upon continuing and important theological questions. There is no effort to achieve agreement or common conclusions, but they look at contemporary issues from the perspective and with the openness of their tradition. For instance, Christopher D. Wiltsher writes on 'Science and Theology from an Arminian Perspective'; Ivor H. Jones adroitly reflects on 'Grace, von Baltha-

sar and the Wesleys'; and Ralph Waller discusses 'The Catholic Spirit: The Need of Our Time'.

All of the essays are significant because their analyses of contemporary issues are full of insight and their use of the resources of the Methodist tradition reveals how fine minds can critically honour their inheritance. There is no space to discuss individual essays. It should be noted, however, that such basic themes as salvation, the Trinity, Christian experience, the Holy Spirit, and theological method are dealt with and that these essays arose out of an ongoing discussion among Methodist theologians. Such discussion reflects the importance of a tradition and contributes to its continuing life [102].

> 102. When a Christian tradition thinks about God it creates possibilities for its own future, and offers a new perspective on its past. This is just the kind of way in which we, by proposing models, try to take responsibility for ourselves. There are many encouragements, in intellectual developments, aesthetic creations, and moral insights in our contemporary society. Is it possible that the Methodist Church could so take responsibility for her past as to make a new future which would serve a wider Christian community and the whole purpose of God for his world?
>
> *Source*: Ivor H. Jones and Kenneth B. Wilson (eds), *Freedom and Grace*, Epworth Press 1988, p. 188.

In a concluding statement, the editors lift up several emphases which are found in the book and which they believe have special importance. First, there is the understanding of God. A suggested model is that the relationship between God and human beings may be conceived in such a manner that there is mutual influence and common creative activity. Secondly, there is the reality of human freedom to the end that human beings can share and manifest the grace of God. There is great cost to self-sharing and in making space for others, but this is what God has done in Jesus Christ and what Christians are called to. Finally, there are developed themes of community as a church and of the community of the church encountering the structures of human society. These themes are all explored in the essays included in the book.

The book is important because it responsibly faces the challenge of speaking to these issues and because it encourages such responsibility within the Methodist tradition. In this regard, it is also in keeping with the other recent Methodist theological contributions described in this chapter.

For discussion

1. From the accounts which Langford gives, who interests you most: John Kent, Kenneth Grayston, David Pailin, Richard Jones or John Stacey? What do you find attractive, illuminating or challenging in what they say?

2. Michael Townsend points to four central emphases of Methodism. Are they central in your local church – or indeed in your own thought?

3. Rupert Davies called his book *What Methodists Believe*. Regarded as a description, is what he says accurate? Regarded as a creed, is it, in any sense, obligatory for Methodist membership?

4. 'Davies wants to bring the creeds to contemporary people; Wainwright wants to bring contemporary people back to the creeds.' Examine the assumptions behind the two approaches. Which do you find more helpful, and why?

5. In what ways should the Methodist Church unite with other Christian churches?

Retrospect and Prospect

We have traced developments in British Methodist theology from its beginnings until the present day [103]. The primary aim has been to follow major trends and search for dominant emphases; and this account, like all others, has not simply recorded events, publications, etc. but has attempted to interpret continuities, divergences and specially important developments. At the same time, while identifying what is shared with other Christian traditions, it has tried to make clear the distinguishing marks of Methodist faith and life.

---

103. Modern Methodists have no Wesley ... nor can they expect to have a Wesley ... This is both a disadvantage and an advantage. The disadvantage is plain enough; the advantage far greater in that Methodists are no longer tied down to one man's interpretation of the Christian faith in all its particulars, enlightened and necessary although that interpretation historically was, and can therefore, if they are so moved by the Spirit, go 'forward from Wesley' into a deeper understanding of God's purpose.

Source: Rupert Davies, 'Methodism Then, and Now', *Epworth Review*, May 1988, p. 26.

Granted the richness and complexity of British Methodist theology, too neat a presentation would certainly have been false and misleading.

British Methodism, a relatively small Christian body, is characterized by: distinguishable forms of worship and small group nurturing; a distinctive hymnody; ministers trained in a range of colleges and courses [104] and participating in the life of an annual Conference; and shared ethical and missionary concerns. To be a Methodist, and certainly to be a Methodist minister, is to be shaped by these factors and in these contexts. One is 'made a Methodist' by participation in the life of this specific community.

---

104. It is clear that in those early days it was recognized that the major part of ministerial training is not determined simply by what is taught in the classroom. Those who teach model the style of ministry. At Hoxton the influence of the Governor, Joseph Entwisle, was vital. He can be seen as the pastor of the whole enterprise using every opportunity to form the character of the students and fit them for their ministry. Tradition thus stated was to continue across the years.

Source: T. T. Rowe, 'One Hundred and Fifty Years of Ministerial Training', *Epworth Review*, January 1985, p. 24.

The transmission of tradition is through this shared life. Continuity is established through apprenticeship, through the influence, conscious or unconscious, of mentors, and through incorporation into and responsibility within the life of this denomination. Though there is teaching, Methodism does not claim a unique understanding of the Christian faith. Within its ethos, the stress is upon mutual support in Christian living.

Methodist tradition, in other words, is conveyed to

every age by ministers and lay people, by congregations and individuals, by schools and teachers, by preachers and social activists, and by congregational singing and service to the needy; and the same multiple and over-lapping media carry it into the next generation. A sense of such a tradition is important, for without the firmness of a tradition criticism has nothing to grasp, and without criticism tradition ceases to have convincing power.

Virginia Woolf, commenting on the novels of Thomas Hardy, notes how inappropriate it is to concentrate on points of detail when Hardy has given us something whose importance does not depend on them. The novels, with their immense range of subject matter, reveal imperfections as well as the marks of genius. When, however, we take them as a whole and recognize their overall achievement, proper appreciation dawns. Perhaps the same applies to the British Methodist theological tradition. Our best understanding does not come from concentration upon small points or particular documents. Rather, as we come to have a sense of the whole, as we gather innumerable clues, as we gain a sense of lives intertwining in worship, fellowship and service, we discover how modes of thought and action, received from parents, are passed to children. Traditions, in the end, are not maintained by argument but by their living power to capture and sustain commitment and vital Christian faith.

Yet, in this as in all religious traditions, there are theological strands, and we have attempted to trace some of their important intellectual and practical aspects, some of their distinctive binding of theory and practice. No special claims for pure intellectual achievement have been or perhaps should be made, but there is room for appropriate pride in, and perhaps thanksgiving for, a tradition which has kept its centre secure and has continually moulded lives in Christian worship, service, and even saintliness.

The British Methodist tradition has been rich. But can it, will it, should it survive? Is there reason and will to ensure its continuance? Time alone will tell. Methodism has certainly fulfilled a significant mission in and through Great Britain. It has made a difference. But, as Methodists have explored ecumenical relations, they have enjoyed shared worship and found themselves largely in agreement with other Christians about fundamental issues such as baptism, eucharist and ministry. They have thus discovered and proudly affirmed this shared faith and mission. The Methodist tradition, to put it another way, has come to understand itself as a stream which, having branched from the broad river of ecumenical Christianity, is now flowing back to rejoin it.

Significant unity within Christ's church is a goal which seems to be coming within reach and grasp, and British Methodism, to judge by its present ecumenical practice and commitment, will enter into union schemes when appropriate opportunities arise; and whenever that happens, the Methodist tradition will enrich the coming church.

The direction, then, is set. But when will uniting begin? Providence cannot be forced, and the time of realizing God's intention waits. In the meantime, British Methodism is called to be faithful to its inheritance, to nurture its special gifts and to keep with humble tenacity the charge it has been given.

For discussion

1. What is likely to be the future of British Methodism?
2. Having read the book, what are your impressions of Methodism and Methodist thought?

Notes

1. The Early Days

1. A word of clarification needs to be entered. The revival movements which eventually joined together (in 1932) to form the Methodist Church in Great Britain did not all trace their origins directly to the Wesleys. Several, coming from the general revivals of the eighteenth and early nineteenth centuries, did not look to the Wesleys as either their founding fathers or their theological mentors. Agreement about general evangelical doctrines of justification by faith, conversion, Christian holiness and the primacy of scripture provided a basic congeniality. But it was a congeniality of parallel movements rather than of varying traditions with the same source. Nevertheless we begin with Wesley because of the formative, if not the exclusive, role he played in the Methodist tradition.

2. On this point see Randy L. Maddox, *Responsible Grace: John Wesley's Practical Theology*, Nashville: Kingswood 1994, p. 17.

   Robert E. Cushman has written: 'We are probably warranted in the judgment that John Wesley, more thoroughly and more cogently than any Christian thinker since St Paul, exposed the vanity, flaccidity, and spiritual facility of an identification of Christian truth and piety with its mere intellectual formulation as creed, or its indoctrination conceived as the way of salvation' (*John Wesley's Experiential Divinity*, Nashville: Kingswood 1989, p. 174).

   H. R. McAdoo has made an important historical point. 'What strikes the moral theologian with fresh force the further he penetrates, is the universal interest of the seventeenth century in "practical divinity" and the importance accorded to it officially and parochially through the period' (*The Structure of Caroline Moral Theology*, London 1949, p. xi). Wesley continued this interest. It was not unique to him but he was important in its embodiment and continuation.

   For a more modest view of Wesley's theological achievement and an interpretation of Wesley without a strong praxis-theory dynamic, see Henry D. Rack, *Reasonable Enthusiast*, Epworth Press, 2nd edn 1992, chapter XI.

3. Stephen Toulmin, 'The Recovery of Practical Philosophy', *The American Scholar*, Summer 1998, p. 338.

4. The word is Heitzenrater's. For a brief and compelling account of the difficulty of capturing the true Wesley, see his chapter, 'The Search for the Real John Wesley' in Richard P. Heitzenrater, *Mirror and Memory*, Nashville: Kingswood 1989, pp. 46–62.

5. For a discussion of this issue, see in Thomas A. Langford (ed), *Doctrine and Theology in the United Methodist Church*, Nashville: Kingswood 1990, articles by Albert C. Outler, 'The Wesleyan Quadrilateral – in John Wesley', pp. 75–90; Ted Campbell, 'The Wesleyan Quadrilateral: The Story of a Modern Methodist Myth', pp. 154–61; and Thomas A. Langford, 'The United Methodist Quadrilateral: A Theological Task', pp. 232–44.

6. In Thomas Jackson, *Lives of Early Methodist Preachers*, London: Conference Office 1865, Vol. II, p. 45: 'In 1770, our Conference was held in London; when Mr Wesley drew up those Minutes which afterwards gave such offence. Had they been seriously considered in the Conference, I am persuaded they would not have been expressed in such an unguarded manner as that in which they appeared. However, the Lord brought great good out of this evil, if so it may be called; for it gave occasion

for the publication of those excellent "checks" of Mr Fletcher, which have afforded many so much edification.'

7. David C. Shipley, 'Methodist Arminianism in the Theology of John Fletcher', Yale University Dissertation 1942, p. 372.

8. See especially Rupert Davies, *Methodism*, Epworth Press, 2nd revd edn 1985 and Thomas A. Langford, *Practical Divinity: Theology in the Wesleyan Tradition*, Nashville: Abingdon 1984, pp. 263f. and more recently Randy L. Maddox, *Responsible Grace*.

9. Albert C. Outler, 'Methodists in Search of Consensus' in *What Should Methodists Teach?*, M. Douglas Meeks (ed), Nashville: Kingswood 1990, p. 37.

10. Geoffrey Wainwright, 'Methodism and the Apostolic Faith' in *What Should Methodists Teach?*, pp. 101–18; Thomas A. Langford, *Practical Divinity*, pp. 262–65.

11. 'Wesley's Place in Church History' in *The Place of Wesley in the Christian Tradition*, Kenneth E. Rowe (ed), Metuchen, NJ: Scarecrow Press 1976, pp. 81–91.

12. *Wesley's Sermons* ed E. H. Sugden, Standard Edition, ii, 342.

13. Ibid.

14. F. Hildebrandt and O. A. Beckerlegge (eds), *A Collection of Hymns for the Use of the People Called Methodists 1780*, OUP 1983, p. xi.

15. On Charles Wesley see, Frank Baker, *Charles Wesley as Revealed by his Letters*, Epworth Press 1948; John R. Tyson, *Charles Wesley: Poet and Theologian* ed S. T. Kimbrough, Jr, Nashville: Kingswood 1992, pp. 97–105; and Richard P. Heitzenrater, 'Early Sermons of John and Charles Wesley' in *Mirror and Memory*, pp. 150–51.

2. *After Wesley*

1. Richard P. Heitzenrater, *Mirror and Memory*, Nashville: Kingswood 1989, pp. 179–80.

2. Ibid., pp. 181–83.

3. Heitzenrater comments that the irony of that decision was that several of Wesley's best doctrinal sermons written in the 1760s were omitted from the sermons which provided the 'standard' of British Methodist doctrine. He then goes on to opine that this struggle with the sermons and the final decision about what is included 'might be seen as one reason why British Methodism today, while still affirming the legal position of Wesley's Sermons and Notes as standards of doctrine, in fact generally ignores Wesley from the pulpit as though he were an embarrassment to modern theological and ecumenical endeavors' (ibid., p. 183).

4. *An Account of The Infancy, Religious and Literary Life of Adam Clarke, Li. D., F.H.S., Etc.*, NY: B. Waugh and T. Mason 1833, p. 10.

5. Ibid.,

6. *Discourses on Various Subjects Related to the Being and Attributes of God*, NY: B. Waugh and T. Mason 1832, Vol. 2, pp. 161–62. For his most complete statement see his 'Autobiography', pp. 95–99 (see n. 4 above) where he lists 32 articles which, he says, came from his study of the Bible. It is this extended creed which he finds completely compatible with dominant Methodist beliefs.

7. *Discourses*, pp. 287–313, Col. 1.27–28.

8. *Discourses*, p. 290.

9. Many of the early Methodist leaders, including theological leaders, were self-made scholars. Characteristic of these persons was their enormous energy and intense discipline. Their achievements were astounding and merit continuing recognition. Adam Clarke, for instance, was a master of perhaps some twenty languages and dialects; he was expert in Arabic and deciphered the Coptic inscriptions on the Rosetta Stone which had puzzled other translators; he was archivist for the British government responsible for collecting materials from the Norman conquest until the accession of George III; he spent some twenty-seven years producing a multi-volume commentary on the entire Bible; he was also a circuit minister and president of the British connection three times and of the Irish connection four times, and he worked constantly for benevolent causes and as a contributor to scholarly journals. One can only stand in awe.

Richard Watson was also remarkable. Thomas Jackson describes him: 'It may give some conception of his activity to survey his labours for the last three years of his life, when he was resident at the City-Road; and they are merely a specimen of his regular and accustomed exertions. During this period he was in a state of constant affliction, and through pain and disease presented almost the appearance of a living skeleton; yet he discharged with efficiency the duties of superintendent of the circuit, except when disabled by illness; he exercised a ministry which increased in interest, and comprehended the delivery of a course of able lectures on the first eight chapters of the Epistle to the Romans; he devoted a part of his time to pastoral visiting from house to house, and especially to visiting the sick; he attended the meetings of the numerous committees entrusted with the management of the Wesleyan book concerns and missions; he spent much time in deliberating with the other secretaries on the affairs of the missions generally, and especially on those of the West Indies, some of which were then violently opposed by the planters and local authorities; during the last of these three years he devoted one forenoon in every week to the missionary work, when he visited Hatton Garden to assist the resident secretaries; he wrote his Conversations for the Young, and his Life of Mr Wesley; he arranged the matter of his Theological and Biblical Dictionary, composed many of its articles, and superintended the printing of the whole; and he also wrote his admirable Exposition of St Matthew's Gospel. Not satisfied with these efforts, he mediated an exposition of the Old Testament, when he had finished the New; and he had entered upon a Life of Mr Charles Wesley, which he intended to pursue as a sort of relaxation from severer studies. Two paragraphs of this work were found in his desk after his decease' (Thomas Jackson, *The Lives of Early Methodist Preachers*, London: Wesleyan Conference Office 1865, Vol. I, p. 466).

10. E. Dale Dunlap, *Methodist Theology in Great Britain in the Nineteenth Century*, Yale University dissertation 1956, p. 98. See also my comments on Watson in *Practical Divinity*, pp. 57–66.

11. Dunlap, op.cit., pp. 212–13.

12. Richard Watson, *Theological Institutes*, John Mason 1846, I, pp. 289–90.

13. *Theological Institutes*, II, pp. 571–72; these are the only references to Wesley.

14. Robert Currie, *Methodism Divided: a study in the sociology of ecumenicalism*, Faber 1968, p. 82.

15. William Arthur, *On the Difference between Physical and Moral Laws*, London 1883, pp. 70–71.

16. John Kent has reinforced awareness of this complexity in his studies in *The Age of Disunity*, Epworth Press 1966.

3. *Methodist Theology in North America*

1. Amplified discussion of the North American situation and the theologians can be found in Thomas A. Langford, *Practical Divinity*, Nashville: Abingdon 1984.

2. There were other spokespersons such as Asa Shinn (1781–1865) and Wilbur Fisk (1792–1839) but they shared Bangs' stance, fighting common enemies and espousing common causes.

3. Phoebe Palmer, *The Way of Holiness and Notes by the Way*, New York: Lane and Scott 1850, pp. 20, 34, 37.

4. It is important to note that in racial attitudes the churches reflected the prevailing cultural and scientific opinions. For an historically significant statement see Melvin Konner, *The Tangled Wing*, New York: Harper Colophon 1983, pp. 439–46.

5. Robert E. Chiles, *Theological Transition in American Methodism 1790–1935*, New York: Abingdon 1965.

6. Albert C. Knudson, 'Henry Clay Sheldon – Theologian', *The Methodist Review*, March 1925, Vol. XLI, pp. 175–92.

7. Ibid., p. 180.

8. Ibid., p. 181.

9. Ibid., p. 187.

10. Again, for an expanded discussion of these developments see Thomas A. Langford, *Practical Divinity*.

11. Edwin Lewis, *A Christian Manifesto*, Nashville: Abingdon 1934.

12. Edwin Lewis, *The Creator and the Adversary*, Nashville: Abingdon 1948.

13. *The Book of Discipline of The United Methodist Church*, Nashville: The United Methodist Publishing House 1992, p. 84. For a thorough discussion of the preparation of this statement, see Richard P. Heitzenrater, 'In Search of Continuity and Consensus: the Road to the 1988 Doctrinal Statement' in Thomas A. Langford, *Doctrine and Theology in the United Methodist Church*, Nashville: Kingswood 1991, pp. 93–108.

14. Methodism, of course, extended far beyond North America, moving both from Britain and from North America. And Methodist Churches around the world have developed theological writings. These traditions are not as old or as independently established as Methodism in North America; nevertheless, it is important, even in a discussion of British Methodist theology, to acknowledge these extensions and to make brief mention of some of the major representatives and developing modes of theology. Methodism in Germany and Switzerland, by the second quarter of the present century, was developing an indigenous statement. Theophil Sporri (1887–1995), a Swiss, taught at the Methodist seminary in Frankfurt, concentrated upon human salvation and God's gracious redemption. Learning from Protestant liberalism, he nevertheless

stressed the evangelical doctrines he had inherited from the Methodist movement. His major work was *Der Mensch und die frohe Botschaft* (3 vols, 1938–1956). Also important are Manfred Marquardt (1940–) who wrote *Praxis und Prinzipien der Sozialethik John Wesley* (Göttingen 1977; Abingdon 1993) and Wilhelm Schneeberger, from Czechoslovakia, who wrote *Theologische Wurzeln des Sozialen Akzents bei John Wesley* (Zurich/Stuttgart 1972). Marquardt joined with Bishop Walter Klaiber to write a systematic theology, *Gelebte Gnade: Grundriss einer Theologie der Evangelisch-Methodistichen Kirche* (Stuttgart 1993).

Other European countries, notably Norway, have produced fine scholars such as Harald Lindstrom, *Wesley and Sanctification* (London 1946); Ole Borgen, *John Wesley and the Sacraments* (Nashville 1972); Thor Hall *The Evolution of Christology* (Nashville 1981), and Peder Borgen, who is a substantial New Testament scholar.

Latin American Methodism has produced a strong voice in liberation theology in José Miguez Bonino, who has written *Christians and Marxists: The Mutual Challenge to Revolution* (Grand Rapids 1976) and *Doing Theology in a Revolutionary Situation* (Philadelphia 1975). Also important are Bishop Mortimer Arias and Ester Arias who wrote *The Cry of My People* (New York 1980).

Asian Methodism has produced Daniel T. Niles of Sri Lanka, a pioneering and important theologian and preacher who wrote, among other things, *A Presentation of the Christian Faith as an Evangelist Would Present it to a Non-Christian* (Calcutta 1956) and *Who is this Jesus?* (Nashville 1968). In the Philippines, Bishop Ernesto Nacpil has been a contributor to theological journals and discussions.

This listing is only suggestive of the wide ranging and growing diversity of Methodist theology. National boundaries are being crossed and contributions are now coming from every area. What began with John Wesley has been enlarged to cover the world.

For a more complete discussion of these developments see Thomas A. Langford, *Practical Divinity*, pp. 239–58; and for discussion of the Disciplinary statements see, Thomas A. Langford (ed), *Doctrine and Theology in The United Methodist Church*, Nashville: Abingdon 1991, pp. 91f.

4. *Times of Change*

1. John Webster Grant, *Freechurchmanship in England, 1870–1940*, London: Independent Press 1962, describes 'the Revolt Against Dogmatic Theology' as a dominant characteristic of Nonconformity at the turn of the century.
2. Ibid., p. 115.
3. Hugh Price Hughes, *Essential Christianity*, New York: Fleming H. Revell Co. 1894, p. 41.
4. Hugh Price Hughes, *Ethical Christianity*, Hodder and Stoughton 1892, p. 14.
5. Hugh Price Hughes, *Essential Christianity*, p. 57.
6. Maldwyn Edwards, *Methodism and England*, Epworth Press 1943, p. 168.
7. *Essential Christianity*, p. 15.
8. B. H. Streeter (ed), *Foundations*, Macmillan 1912.
9. Virginia Woolf, 'Mr Bennett and Mrs Brown', *The Hogarth Essays*, Hogarth Press 1924, pp. 4–5.
10. Herbert Read, *Contemporary British Art*, Penguin Books, revd edn 1964, p. 20.
11. C. M. Bowra, *The Background of Modern Poetry*, Clarendon Press 1954, pp. 3, 5–6, 8.
12. Arnold Bennett, 'The Religious Interregnum' in *Affirmations*, collected by Ernest Benn Ltd 1929, p. 10.
13. E. H. Carr in *Conditions of Peace*, Macmillan 1942, quoted in A. J. P. Taylor, *English History 1914–1945*, Clarendon Press 1965, p. 299.
14. Francis Boyd, *British Politics in Transition 1945–53*, New York: Praeger 1964, pp. 13–14.
15. Quoted in M. B. Reckitt, *Maurice to Temple*, Faber 1947, p. 208.
16. The lines are from an early poem, *The Orators*, which Auden later withdrew from publication. They are quoted by C. Day-Lewis in *A Hope for Poetry*, Blackwell 1934, p. 45.
17. B. H. Streeter in *Foundations*, pp. vii–viii.
18. Gordon Wakefield, 'Methodist Union: Youthful Memories, Adult Assessment and Future Hopes', *Epworth Review*, May 1982, p. 30.

5. *Scripture, Experience, Atonement*

1. John Kent, *The Age of Disunity*, Epworth Press 1966, p. 9.
2. Kent, op.cit., p. 21.
3. Quoted in Kent, op.cit., p. 21.
4. Kent, op.cit., p. 21.

5. In *A History of the Methodist Church in Great Britain*, Vol. 3, Epworth Press 1983, p. 213.

6. H. Maldwyn Hughes, *The Theology of Experience*, Epworth Press 1915, p. 11.

7. Ibid., pp. 236–37.

8. John Scott Lidgett, *The Spiritual Principle of the Atonement*, Epworth Press 1897, p. 484.

9. John McLeod Campbell, *The Nature of the Atonement*, 2nd edn 1867, p. xvii.

10. F. D. Maurice, *Theological Essays* (1853), Essay VII.

11. B. F. Westcott, *The Victory of the Cross* (1888), pp. 78, 83.

12. Horace Bushnell, *Vicarious Sacrifice* (1866), p. 11.

13. Albrecht Ritschl, *Justification and Reconciliation* (1872), vol. III, 259.

14. John Scott Lidgett, *The Spiritual Principle of the Atonement*, p. 218.

15. Ibid., p. 219.

16. Ibid., p. 414.

17. W. R. Maltby, 'The Meaning of the Cross', *Manuals of Fellowship* pamphlet No. 10, Epworth Press n.d. (c. 1926), p. 2.

18. C. Ryder Smith, *The Bible Doctrine of Salvation*, Epworth Press 1941, p. 10.

19. Ibid., p. 310.

20. Ibid., p. 310.

21. Ibid., p. 310.

22. Vincent Taylor, *The Atonement in New Testament Teaching*, Epworth Press 1940, pp. 167–71.

23. Ibid., p. 198.

24. The doctrine of the atonement provides an available entry point to the general area of the study of non-Christian religions and inter-faith dialogue. Methodists have made significant contributions to both of these areas. Professor E. Geoffrey Parrinder is the single most significant Methodist in the study of other religions in the twentieth century. Since the 1950s he has published work on African, Asian and world religions. Learned and prolific, he has provided much of the material for succeeding interpreters.

   Other scholars have also been interested and there is currently much attention to the subject. We shall see in the work of John Stacey an assumption about the universality of religion and suggestions as to how this awareness must be taken into account by theological interpretation. Other aspects of possible relationships are explored by Martin Forward, of Wesley House Cambridge, who believes that the discussion should be shifted from soteriology to christology; while W. Roy Pape, who once served in south India and is now a Methodist minister in Leicestershire, sees christology and soteriology closely intertwined and argues that the love of God expressed in the cross cannot be subservient to the historical happening of the cross.

   A representation of the present discussion may be found in Westminster Wesley Series, No. 3, Summer 1995, *Pure, Universal Love*. Other important publications are Kenneth Cracknell, *Towards A New Relationship* (Epworth Press 1986) and *Justice, Courtesy and Love: Theologians and Missionaries Encountering World Religions 1846–1914* (Epworth Press 1995); Martin Forward (ed), *God of All Faith: Discerning God's Presence in Multi-Faith Society* (London 1989), and *Ultimate Visions, One World* (Oxford 1996); Frank Whaling, *Christian Theology and World Religions* (Marshall Pickering 1986); and the Methodist Church, *Statements of the Methodist Church on Faith and Order 1933–83*, 'Relations with People of Other Faiths' (London 1984).

6. *Holiness, Church, Practical Theology*

1. John Wesley, *Letters*, Standard Edition ed J. Telford, Epworth Press 1931, viii, 238.

2. T. & T. Clark 1917, ix, pp. 718–37.

3. Henry D. Rack, *The Future of John Wesley's Methodism*, Lutterworth Press 1965, p. 34.

4. W. E. Sangster, *The Pure in Heart*, Epworth Press 1954, p. 196.

5. Ibid., p. 239.

6. William Strawson, 'Methodist Theology 1850–1950' in Rupert Davies, A. Raymond George and Gordon Rupp (eds), *A History of The Methodist Church in Great Britain*, Vol. 3, Epworth Press 1983, pp. 192–93.

7. R. Newton Flew, *Jesus and His Church*, Epworth Press 1938, p. 264.

7. *Contemporary Trends*

1. These comments are made on the basis of John Kent's *The End of the Line?*, SCM Press 1982.

2. Ibid., p. 16.

3. Ibid., p. 19.

4. Richard G. Jones, *Groundwork of Christian Ethics*, Epworth Press 1984, p. 54.

5. Ibid., pp. 221–22.

6. John Stacey, *Groundwork of Theology*, Epworth Press 1984, p. 178.

7. Ibid., p. 253.

8. Rupert E. Davies, *Religious Authority in an Age of Doubt*, Epworth Press 1968, p. 33.

9. Ibid., pp. 207–8.

10. Ibid., p. 219.

11. Rupert E. Davies, *What Methodists Believe*, Mowbray 1976, p. 19. Important as background is Davies' chapter, 'The People called Methodist: i, "Our Doctrines"' in *A History of the Methodist Church in Great Britain*, Vol. 1, pp. 147–79. In this chapter he explicates John Wesley's thought without extensive editorial commentary.

12. Ibid., p. 84.

13. Rupert E. Davies, *Making Sense of the Creeds*, Epworth Press 1987, p. 12.

14. Ibid., pp. 47–48.

15. Ibid., p. 84.

16. Ibid., pp. 84–85.

17. Geoffrey Wainwright, *Methodists in Dialog*, Abingdon 1995, pp. 277–78.

18. Ibid., pp. 17–18.

19. Ibid., pp. 271, 279f.

20. *Churches Respond to BEM*, Geneva, 1986–88, Vol. 2, pp. 230–35.

21. Ivor H. Jones and Kenneth B. Wilson (eds), *Freedom and Grace*, Epworth Press 1988, p. 111.

Select Bibliography

containing, except in the case of the last three chapters (see below), details of all works mentioned in the text but not quoted, plus other books which, together with those cited in the footnotes, will be useful for Further Reading.

Chapter 1

John Wesley

Standard Editions of:
Sermons (2 vols), ed E. H. Sugden, Epworth Press, 4th edn 1955–56.
Journal (8 vols), ed Nehemiah Curnock, Epworth Press 1909–16.
Letters (8 vols), ed John Telford, Epworth Press 1931.

A 'Bicentennial Edition' of Wesley's Works began appearing in 1975, first published by OUP and more recently by Abingdon Press. When complete, this will be the fullest and most accurate text of Wesley's works ever to be published.

Albert C. Outler (ed), *John Wesley*, OUP 1964. The best one-volume selection of Wesley's writings.
V. H. H. Green, *John Wesley*, Nelson 1964. The best short biography.
Henry D. Rack, *Reasonable Enthusiast: John Wesley and the Rise of Methodism*, 2nd edn, Epworth Press 1992. Likely to remain the standard biography for some years.
Colin W. Williams, *John Wesley's Theology Today*, Epworth Press 1960. A useful summary of Wesley's thought.

John Fletcher of Madeley

Collected Works (8 vols), John Mason 1836–38.
George Lawton, *Shropshire Saint: A Study in the Ministry and Spirituality of Fletcher of Madeley*, Wesley Historical Society Lecture no. 26, Epworth Press 1960. A very good introduction.

Peter S. Forsaith, *The Eagle and the Dove: John Fletcher, vicar of Madeley – towards a new assessment*, Bristol, the author 1979.

Luke Tyerman, *Wesley's Designated Successor: the Life, Letters and Literary Labours of the Revd John William Fletcher, Vicar of Madeley, Shropshire*, Hodder and Stoughton 1882. Valuable, despite its age, because Tyerman is always remarkably accurate.

P. P. Streiff, *John William Fletcher 1729–85*, Peter Lang 1984. The best book on Fletcher but in German.

Charles Wesley

John Capon, *John and Charles Wesley: the preacher and the poet*, Hodder and Stoughton 1988.

Journal and selections of correspondence and poetry, ed Thomas Jackson (2 vols), John Mason 1849.

John Vickers, *Charles Wesley*, Foundery Press 1990. A brief but most useful 'way in' for the student of Charles.

F. C. Gill, *Charles Wesley, the First Methodist*, Lutterworth Press 1964. A scholarly but readable biography.

Frank Baker, *Charles Wesley as Revealed by his Letters*, Epworth Press 1948.

John Lawson, *A Thousand Tongues: the Wesley Hymns as a Guide to Scriptural Teaching*, Paternoster 1987. Perhaps the best recent introduction to the theology of Charles' hymns.

J. Ernest Rattenbury, *The Evangelical Doctrines of Charles Wesley's Hymns*, Epworth Press 1941. A major study which has become a classic.

Rupert Davies, A. Raymond George and Gordon Rupp (eds), *A History of the Methodist Church in Great Britain*, Epworth Press 1965–1988, offers three volumes of historical essays and a final volume of documents and bibliography. Volume I covers the beginnings of Methodism and contains essays on John and Charles Wesley and an appendix to the chapter on 'Our Doctrines' on John Fletcher's contribution to the Antinomian controversy (see pp. 176–79).

The short account of the emergence of Methodism in Gordon Rupp's *Religion in England 1688–1791*, OUP 1986, pp. 325–493 is also commended.

Chapter 2

Adam Clarke

Commentary on the Bible (8 vols), Butterworth 1825.

Christian Theology, London 1835.

Discourses on Various Subjects Related to the Being and Attributes of God, New York: Waugh and Mason 1832.

An Account of the Infancy, Religious and Literary Life of Adam Clarke Ll.D., F.A.S. etc., New York: Waugh and Mason 1833.

Maldwyn Edwards, *Adam Clarke*, Wesley Historical Society lecture no. 8, Epworth Press 1942.

Richard Watson

Theological Institutes, 1826, 7th edn, John Mason 1846.
Biblical and Theological Dictionary, 1833.
Life of Mr Wesley, John Mason 1831.
Edward J. Brailsford, *Richard Watson: theologian and missionary advocate*, Charles Kelly 1906.

William Arthur

The Tongue of Fire, 1856, centenary edition, abridged by John H. J. Barker, Epworth Press 1956.
On the Difference between Physical and Moral Law, 1883.
Religion without God and *God without Religion*, 1885–88: initially in 3 parts.
Norman W. Taggart, *William Arthur: first among Methodists*, Epworth Press 1993.

William Burt Pope

The Person of Christ, 1871.
A Compendium of Christian Theology, 1875; 3 vol. edn 1880.
Higher Catechism of Theology, 1883.
Sermons:
Sermons, Addresses and Charges, 1878.
Discourses, chiefly on the Lordship of the Incarnate Redeemer, 1880.
Inward Witness and other Discourses, 1885.
[All Pope's books were published by the Wesleyan Methodist Conference Office/ Book Room]
R. Waddy Moss, *W. B. Pope DD: Theologian and Saint*, Culley, n.d./?1906.

Chapter 3

Thomas A. Langford, *Practical Divinity: Theology in the Wesleyan Tradition*, Abingdon 1983.
Thomas A. Langford, *Wesleyan Theology: a sourcebook*, The Labyrinth Press 1984.
Nathan Bangs, *The Errors of Hopkinsianism*, privately printed, 1815.
Nathan Bangs, *Predestination Examined*, 1817.
Nathan Bangs, *The Present State and Prospects, and Responsibilities of the Methodist Episcopal Church*, New York: Lane and Scott 1850.
Abel Stevens, *Life and Times of Nathan Bangs DD*, New York: Carlton and Foster 1863.

Phoebe Palmer, *The Way of Holiness and Notes by the Way*, New York: Lane and
    Scott 1851. 1st British edn 1856.
Randolf S. Foster, *Christian Purity*, New York: Eaton and Mains 1869, 2nd edn
    1897.
Thomas O. Summers, *Systematic Theology*, 2 vols, ed J. J. Tigert: Nashville:
    Methodist Episcopal Church, South, Publishing House 1888.
John Miley, *Systematic Theology*, 2 vols, New York: Hunt and Easton 1893.
Henry Clay Sheldon, *Unbelief in the Nineteenth Century*, New York: Eaton and
    Main 1907.
Henry Clay Cheldon, *The Essentials of Christianity*, 1922.
Borden Parker Bowne, *Atonement*, Cincinnati: Jennings and Pye/New York: Eaton
    and Main 1900.
Borden Parker Bowne, *The Essence of Religion* (Sermons), Boston/New York:
    Houghton and Mifflin Co. 1910.
Francis J. McConnell, *Borden Parker Bowne*, Nashville/New York: Cokesbury
    Press 1929.
Albert C. Knudson, *The Validity of Religious Experience*, Nashville: Cokesbury
    Press 1937.
Albert C. Knudson, *The Doctrine of God*, Nashville: Cokesbury Press 1930.
Albert C. Knudson, *The Doctrine of Redemption*, Nashville: Cokesbury Press
    1933.
Albert C. Knudson, *The Philosophy of Personalism*, Boston 1927.
Edwin Lewis, *A Christian Manifesto*, Nashville: Cokesbury Press 1934.
Edwin Lewis, *A Philosophy of the Christian Revelation*, Harper and Brothers
    1940; Epworth Press 1948.
Umphrey Lee, *John Wesley and Modern Religion*, Nashville: Cokesbury Press 1936.
Harald Lindstrom, *Wesley and Sanctification: a study in the doctrine of salvation*,
    Epworth Press 1950.
William R. Cannon, *The Theology of John Wesley, with special reference to the
    doctrine of justification*, New York: Abingdon–Cokesbury 1946.
For details of the writings of Frank Baker, Albert C. Outler and Robert
E. Cushman, see Thomas A. Langford, *Practical Divinity*, Abingdon 1983; and
for selections from the last two, see Thomas A. Langford, *Wesleyan Theology: a
sourcebook*, The Labyrinth Press 1984.
John B. Cobb Jr., *God and the World*, Philadelphia: Westminster Press 1969.
John B. Cobb Jr., *A Christian Natural Theology*, Philadelphia: Westminster Press
    1965.
John B. Cobb Jr., *The Structure of Christian Existence*, Lutterworth 1968.
John B. Cobb Jr., *Process Theology as Political Theology*, Manchester University
    Press/Westminster Press 1982.
David Ray Griffin and Thomas J. J. Altizer (eds), *John Cobb's Theology in
    Process*, Westminster Press 1977.
Schubert M. Ogden, *Christ without Myth*, Collins 1962.
Schubert M. Ogden, *The Reality of God*, SCM Press 1967.

Schubert M. Ogden, *The Point of Christology*, SCM Press 1982.
Schubert M. Ogden, *Faith and Freedom*, Nashville: Abingdon 1979.

Chapter 4

Hugh Price Hughes

Social Christianity, Hodder and Stoughton 1889.
The Philanthropy of God, Hodder and Stoughton 1890.
Ethical Christianity, Hodder and Stoughton 1892.
Dorothea Price Hughes, *The Life of Hugh Price Hughes*, Hodder and Stoughton 1904.
A. J. Ayer, *Language, Truth and Logic*, Gollancz 1936; 2nd edn 1948; now in Pelican.
William Temple, *Nature, Man and God*, Macmillan 1934.
Leslie D. Weatherhead, *The Will of God*, Epworth Press 1944 and many reprints.

Since a great number of books are mentioned in chapters 5–7, invariably with the place of publication, there seems little point in listing them, simply to add the publisher. For these chapters, therefore, a list of useful background books is offered.

Chapter 5

H. K. Moulton (ed), *James Hope Moulton*, Epworth Press 1963.
W. F. Lofthouse and others, *Wilbert F. Howard*, Epworth Press 1954.
John T. Wilkinson, *Arthur Samuel Peake*, Epworth Press 1971.
For an appreciation of Vincent Taylor, see the introductory essays to Vincent Taylor, *New Testament Essays*, Epworth Press 1970, pp. 1–30.

John Scott Lidgett

The Spiritual Principle of the Atonement, Sharp 1897.
The Fatherhood of God, 1902.
The Christian Religion: its meaning and proof, 1907.
The Victorian Transformation of Theology, Epworth Press 1934.
My Guided Life, Methuen 1936.
R. E. Davies (ed), *John Scott Lidgett*, Epworth Press 1957.

Chapter 6

For William Arthur and W. B. Pope, see under *Chapter 1* above.
G. S. Wakefield, *Robert Newton Flew 1886–1962*, Epworth Press 1971.
P. Sangster, *Dr Sangster*, Epworth Press 1962.

Chapter 7

To the series of Groundwork Books have been added:
Diarmaid MacCulloch, *Groundwork of Christian History*, Epworth Press 1987.
Susan J. White, *Groundwork of Christian Worship*, Epworth Press 1997,
and volumes on Science and Religion, Christian Approach to Other Religions,
Theology of Mission and Pastoral Theology are in preparation.

Index

40319186R00070

Made in the USA
Middletown, DE
09 February 2017